A Blend of
Contradictions

A Blend of Contradictions

Georg Simmel in Theory and Practice

Ann-Mari Sellerberg

Transaction Publishers
New Brunswick (U.S.A.) and London (U.K.)

Library of Congress Catalog Number: 93-19449
ISBN: 1-56000-120-8
Printed in the United States of America

Library of Congress Cataloging-in-Publication Data

Sellerberg, Ann-Mari, 1943-
    A blend of contradictions: Georg Simmel in theory and practice/Ann-Mari Sellerberg.
      p.   cm.
    Includes bibliographical references and index.
    ISBN 1-56000-120-8 (cloth)
      1. Simmel, Georg, 1858-1918. 2. Sociology—Germany—History. I. Title.
HM22.G3S493   1993
301'.092dc20   93-19449
                                                                CIP

Contents

Acknowledgements

First of all, I wish to thank my family for all the support and inspiration they have given me over the years. My husband, Rune Persson, a fellow sociologist, utilizes a very different approach from mine, but still gave constant encouragement; and my five children — in a way known to every parent — dragged me into the most variegated experiences which coloured some parts of my interview investigations.

My thanks are also due to Malin Åkerström for the wonderful asset of a colleague who is sufficiently like as well as unlike myself, in respect of lines of thought as well as lines of research, and with whom I found I could discuss everything, stimulated by just the right measure of dissimilarity. I am grateful, too, to Fabian Persson, who assisted in the typing of the manuscript, and to Marianne Thormählen, who helped with the English translation — and with so many other things.

The Swedish Council for Research in the Humanities and Social Sciences kindly provided a generous grant for preparing the English text, a much-appreciated contribution.

Two chapters constitute revised versions of previously published articles. Thus, Chapter 8 ("Subordination under a Principle: Interactions in Geriatric Hospitals") is a reworked version of an article entitled "Expressivity within a time schedule," published in *Sociology of Health & Illness* 13.1 (1990); and Chapter 10 ("The Poor of Our Time: Objects of Enlightened Despotism") is a revised version of "Nutritional Norms in Long-term Care Analyzed from a Simmelean Perspecitve," *Acta Sociologica* 1989 (32), pp 275-282, published by Scandinavian University Press, Oslo.

Preface

The marvellous thing about the classics is the plain and lucid way in which they communicate themselves to subsequent generations. This does not mean that their messages are always the same; on the contrary, their words may be differently interpreted and come to assume very specific significance to each of us, depending on our own personal experiences.

My own background is that of the empiricist. From the 1960s onwards, I have been performing both quantitative and qualitative investigations of a great variety of subjects: the mothers of small children, living in housing estates (high-rise buildings) and distressed at the way in which architects had introduced "holistic solutions" in their appartments (removing doors, in other words); anger directed against women in service jobs; the ideas of overweight hypertensives about food; and different tastes in respect of interior decoration, clothes, food, and first names for children. I have examined the holiday activities of young girls and performed taped interviews in order to find out what geriatric patients talk about during meals; at the moment I am investigating bankruptcy as social behaviour. Clearly, then, I am a bit of a "general dealer" in the field of sociology.

Once I have submitted my empirical reports, however, I have always made a point of trying to find time to ponder the empirical results. How might the analysis be continued? After all, even the most trivial and matter-of-fact can be made to serve as a basis for the application of the old Flemish proverb quoted by Simmel, "There is more within me."

During these cogitations, the sociology of Georg Simmel has been my constant companion. It contains inexhaustible reserves of insights, many of them untapped or — as one Simmel scholar has pointed out — tapped in secret, often expressed in acute observations of the complex relationships that characterize human existence. For instance, Simmel shows that subordination does not always amount to being subordinated in every respect, and that a role which demands everything from us also forces us to step outside it. In real life, every trust is a shaky process constantly accompanied by distrust; and the calculated portion of discovery that forms part of present-day package-tour holidays stands out more clearly when contrasted with the "adventure" described by Simmel. What, one may wonder, does it actually feel like to be at the receiving end of current social services, to be a kind of social-security recipient, built into a program with handsomely-defined purposes? Do these people, the poor of our time, become the objects of enlightened despotism? Do they in fact turn into instruments geared to fulfilling the purposes of the program? If so, the recipient of social service may also become an annoying obstacle blocking the realization of those purposes.

Time and again, I have found that Simmel's observations may well be applied by an empiricist who wishes to analyze his/her material, even if that material is very much bound up with the present-day situation. Besides, those observations are expressed in an incredibly striking, and indeed enjoyable, manner in his works - not only in the major essays but also in newspaper articles, aphorisms, and letters.

I would be glad if this book could do something to indicate the range of opportunities opened by Simmel's sociology to the empirically orientated researcher, who need not confine himself/herself to the established "Simmel areas" such as conflict, trust, secrets, etc. There is such abundance in his work and such constant pertinence.

This book deliberately moves on rather a special level. A reader who expects empirical accounts will be as disappointed as the person who looks for theoretical argument. My perspective is that of continued wonderment at human society and at the phenomena I have myself described empirically. What does it all signify in the end?

Introduction

A Blend of Contradictions

Contradiction forms the basis of all social phenomena. Look for contradiction, and finding it you will perceive something of vital importance. This is a fundamental conception in Simmel's writings. He serves as an illuminator of the essential contradictoriness which characterizes social phenomena.

Simmel's knowledge of the world thus turns out to be of a very particular kind. It is never a matter of causal understanding. Instead, Simmel criticizes this kind of knowledge:

> We think we actually understand things only when we have traced them back to what we do not understand and cannot understand - to causality, to axioms, to God, to character. (Simmel's diary cited by Wolff 1964, p. xxi)

Simmel "breaks down" social phenomena into isolated categories — and in these categories he discerns powers, energies, and tendencies working in "pairs"; each one is inevitably associated with its opposite. These pairs seem to function together in a dual fashion — they hinder and inhibit as well as reinforce and strengthen each other.

We are constantly seeking ultimate forces, fundamental aspirations, some one of which controls our entire mode of behavior. But in no case do we find any single force attaining a perfectly independent expression, and we are thus obliged to separate a majority of factors and determine the relative extent to which each shall be represented. To do this we must establish the degree of limitation exercised by the counteraction of some other force, as well as the influence exerted by the latter upon the primitive force (Levine 1971, p. xxxv).

Simmel's manner of writing is always based on this particular knowledge: phenomena *are* contradictions, they *are* syntheses of particular opposing forces (Moreland 1978).

It could, however, also be said that social phenomena tend — by their very nature — to conceal their inherent contradictions. Man has always had a dualistic nature; this fact has had but little effect on the uniformity of his conduct. Simmel emphasizes that "... this uniformity is usually the result of a number of elements. An action that results from less than a majority of fundamental forces would appear barren and empty" (Simmel 1973, p. 171).

In Practice

Simmel in practice simply denotes an application of this knowledge of the presence of dualistic forces and mutual tensions to extremely concrete, everyday, and ubiquitous social phenomena. Hence, my point of departure is precisely the Simmelean element which has been said to have had little influence in the US (Levine et al 1976). Most of the American literature on Simmel's sociology has been limited to Simmel's "forms of sociation" (sociability, domination, subordination, marginality). Debates regarding the ontological status of "forms" have been going on for a long time (Zerubavel 1981b). By contrast, these basic dialectical aspects of Simmel's thinking have often been screened out by people trained in American modes of thought, where the univocal and one-dimensional tends to prevail (Levine et al 1976).

Maybe these empirical analyses in the spirit of Simmel will therefore appear speculative in that specifically European way which Merton discerned when he wrote about the "European species" versus the "American species" of sociology (Merton 1957). Conceivably, the essays may confront the supposed difficulty experienced by American sociologists when dealing with Simmel's ambiguities and with his dualistic conceptions.

It has often been pointed out that Simmel's perspective is a very special one. He assumes a unique attitude to the world. Still, "perspective" and "attitude" do not seem to me to be satisfactory designations in this context. First, these terms imply seeing something from a certain viewpoint, surveying things from a certain position. The words suggest distance, without a hint of proximity. Second — and this may be even more important — these words imply passive behavior. "Attitude" and "perspective" create an impression of passive "armchair interpretation" performed from a distance. Third, stressing a certain perspective suggests a concomitant lack of interest in empirical realities.

After all, we are not dealing with a mere "perspective," but with knowledge of the world. This knowledge of social phenomena calls for a certain method. It presupposes closeness and distance at the same time. Simmel expresses this doubleness in his analytical interpretations of the world. It is a somewhat tragicomical fact that closeness — the multitude of the concrete — should be so confusing, whereas distance in its abstractness and relative emptiness produces a feeling of clearness and insight precisely because of its lack of empirical content (Welander 1972). According to Simmel, though, knowledge must encompass both.

Actually, every Simmelean analysis is charged with empirical matter. In this study, I have wanted to draw attention to the empirical possibilities inherent in discerning the contradictoriness that is characteristic of every social phenomenon. Opposite tendencies explain — in fact, *are* — social life.

Simmel has often been regarded as the truly un-empirical formalist. It is claimed that formal sociology "ever since the days of its founder Georg Simmel, ... has usually been associated with the armchair and the library. It has been looked upon as divorced from any direct contact with social reality" (Zerubavel 1981b, p. 25). But separate non-empirical "forms," in Simmel's sense of the word, are inconceivable. Empirically, we can never isolate form or content as a distinct entity. They constitute — or, rather, their empirical counterparts constitute — the unity of one and the same reality.

Consequently, any analytical category must always be anchored in everyday life, because only in this way can content be realized socially by way of a particular form. This, too, is the only way in which form is socially realized through a particular content. The same thing may be said about science and knowledge. An interaction of two motives develops — utilitarian knowledge and knowledge for its own sake. One must never quite take the place of the other. To Simmel, knowledge is also — and, always, originally — a practical instrument. Its origin and motive function as a weapon in man's struggle for survival. However, knowledge invariably becomes an end in itself as well.

Methodological Interactionism

Every sociological method demands that we recognize — in every moment of existence — a pair of forces, each one of which, in striving to go beyond the initial point, has resolved the infinity of the other by mutual impingement into mere tension and desire (Simmel 1973).

In point of fact, Simmel's method might be described as "methodological interactionism." This term is adequate in a double sense: Not only are the social categories which Simmel analyzes different types of interactions; they are also analyzed as interactions of interactions. These are interactions of a different order - an order which is dialectical. — In the following chapters, by way of various empirical applications, I attempt to illustrate and illuminate three different ways in which these opposed forces affect each other.

- The first section is concerned with the way in which a special conflict, or special conflicts, characterize a social phenomenon. In fact, the element of opposition may, in sociological terms, be said to *be* this phenomenon. In this section, I deal with such matters as modern motherhoood, women in typical women's occupations, trust, and the interest of geriatric patients in expressing individualism — albeit in a restrained form — in the patient groups who spend their days in the living-rooms of geriatric institutions.

- The special (characteristic) opposing tendencies in the phenomenon become a motor and an impetus to continuous change. Coser writes:

  Attempts to analyze social action without reference to the reactions which it calls forth and which condition further action would have been rejected by Simmel as examples of what he called the *fallacy of separateness*. (Coser 1965, p. 13)

- The interactions of contradictory forces constantly tend toward the ironic and the paradoxical. This, to Simmel, amounts to a virutally inescapable logic. Human beings create various things in accordance with their intentions and their most intense desires. What they have created, however, assumes an objective form and follows an immanent logic of development, becoming alienated from its origin as well as from its purpose (Simmel 1923, p. 260).

To Be and Not To Be: The Contradiction is the Thing

Unlike most modern sociologists, the great sociologists of the past always stressed the idea that social action is rarely founded upon single unambiguous interests. Social actors frequently find themselves caught up in a Weberian struggle of motives, which leads to an irresolvable conflict (Weber 1968a, p. 10). Whichever side prevails in this battle, the orientation of the action around one set of interests necessarily takes place at the expense of the side that has lost. Whatever action an individual takes, one element in his/her motive gives priority to the suppressed interests at the next available opportunity. This, in turn, damages the first interest, and so on.

To modify Shakespeare: To be or not to be is not the question, but to be and not to be (Welander 1972). This duality is the category or principle which makes individuals into a concrete society: Thus, no individual belongs *wholly* to a certain social category — *and* the outside part is never separated from the inside part. A basic example: The individual must be social in order to be non-social — and non-social in order to be social. This is our extra-social nature, which characterizes all of us and also distinguishes every social relation. Simmel writes:

> The "within" and the "without" between individual and society are not two unrelated definitions but define together the fully homogenous position of man as a social animal. (Simmel 1965, p. 350)

Any dynamic structure consists of opposing forces and tendencies. Both are always present; parallel to any involvement, for instance, there exists a restraining tendency affecting this very same involvement and interest.

Concord, harmony, co-efficacy, which are unquestionably held to be socializing forces, must nevertheless be interspersed with distance, competition, repulsion, in order to yield the actual configuration of society. (Simmel 1964, p. 315)

The Oppositions within a Phenomenon become a Motor, inducing Change

Simmel uses the metaphor of the circle or curve to describe one of the ways in which the processes of social interactions unfold.

> If the effect that one element produces upon another then becomes a cause that reflects back as an effect upon the former, which in turn repeats the process by becoming a cause of retroaction, then we have a model of genuine infinity in activity. Here is an immanent infinity comparable to that of the circle. . . (Simmel 1978, p. 119)

Nedelmann writes that her purpose is to demonstrate that Simmel's approach, and concise analysis of the world of fashion, do not merely constitute an exotic contribution to the sociology of aesthetics. Instead, they contribute to the general theory of social action — or, to put it more precisely, to the theory of *Eigendynamik* or autonomous processes of social interaction (See Nedelmann 1987, p. 2.).

Scholars have occasionally directed their attention towards this type of circular social-interaction processes that has been described by Simmel (see Nedelmann 1987). They have not, however, considered the potential significance of this metaphor where the general theory of social action is concerned. Taking the metaphor of the circle at face value would entail a withdrawal from the causal approach — it would mean that sociologists stopped regarding phenomena as developing unidirectionally, from cause to effect. It would call for the realisation that cause and effect might reverse roles in the course of processes of interaction.

A particularly vital point is made by Nedelmann: If we accept that the processes of social interaction can unfold in a way which is analogous to the formation of a circle, this would imply that these processes create their own momentum; they are, to use a term which is difficult to translate, *eigendynamisch* (Mayntz & Nedelmann 1987).

Simmel pursued this fundamental insight in considerable depth. He saw social life as a "battle ground, of which every inch is stubbornly contested" (Simmel 1971, p. 296). In social interaction, people try to satisfy their needs for rest *and* movement, integration *and* isolation, opposition *and* obedience, freedom *and* obligation (to name some of the examples mentioned by Simmel). The important thing is that it is these contradictions, the obstruction *and* reinforcement of forces, that unleash processes which gain their own momentum. These forces continue indefinitely because the structure of needs is by definition irresolvable.

Paradoxes — the Ironies of Social Life

It is often claimed that Simmel concentrated on a micro-level. Most of his analyses are concerned with intimate, unspoken feelings — with trust, closeness, gratitude, faithfulness. In my view, though, this element of everyday intimacy is not in fact the heart of the matter. Instead, the vital issue is that these phenomena are made up of those interactions of contradictory forces which are forever tending towards the paradoxical.

The point I want to make is that whenever trust, gratitude, adventure etc. are concerned, what we aim for and desire must, basically, follow in the manner of a "by-product." In such matters as these, what we are striving for can never be made to happen by any amount of planning or coercion; if we try, it is transformed into its opposite. The most important things, the most hotly desired ones, must always be by-products, secondary phenomena created as it were off-stage.

Trust, adventure, intimacy, and fashion cannot be produced to order, planned, or governed. With regard to trust, for instance, the moment when we make an effort to appear truly trusting, or try hard to gain someone's confidence, the opposite effect is always engendered. Fashion is the same; it has to be incalculable. In spite of all fashion agencies, there are no such things as guarantees in fashion. One might say the same thing about holiday adventures; the unexpected can never be ensured in advance. Still, human enterprise consists in perpetual endeavours in these various directions. After all, we do try to ensure confidence, plan for the fashions of the future, make sure that our adventurous holiday will happen...

This is a vital basic theme with Simmel: social life is inevitably ironic. That's life. What we really want, and are anxious to secure, in terms of social life is thwarted in consequence of our very efforts.

Simmel helps us perceive life's little ironies everywhere: We strive, desire, and establish institutions for certain purposes — but they are ineluctably removed from what they were intended for and start leading a life divorced from — and opposed to — their origins.

Conclusion

Simmel has been criticized for devoting special attention to phenomena at the micro-level. It has been claimied that what he analyzes is not, after all, of any great consequence. Actually, though, the micro-phenomena he investigates are always among us. They have to do with what is common to virtually all human beings — trust, intimacy, marginality, all omnipresent things. And they have consequences: in the end, for instance, trust or distrust is decisive in relations between human beings.

I regard Simmel's interest in the micro-level as expressing an endeavour to move in really closely — an endeavour which *cannot* be viewed as a matter of "perspective."

To my mind, this endeavour — despite the "armchair" epithet — embodies a certain empirical tenacity. Micro- and macro-levels, specificity *and* generality — such planes become meaningless. Distance *and* closeness are always inherent in the interrelations of things. Every area, every level, must be accessible to analysis.

Furthermore, it is mandatory that each analysis proceed from its special empirical content: What opposed forces and contradictions are characteristic of a particular phenomenon? It is not, for example, possible to assume "in advance" that a certain form can be applied to areas such as holidays, the gainful labor of women, or trust in an urban context.

Simmel summarizes his basic conception according to which the analysis should always be taken a step further — what was referred to above as "empirical tenacity" — by quoting the inscription on an old Flemish house: "There is more within me" (Simmel 1973, p. 171). This, too, is the formula according to which every initial and necessarily fragmentary analysis of a social phenomenon ought to proceed.

I

To Be *and* Not to Be:
The Contradiction Is the Thing

1

Modern Motherhood

Only by experiencing a state as being restricted can you go beyond its restrictions. This recognition forms the point of departure for an analysis of what it means to be a mother in Sweden today.

My reasoning is based on an investigation among young Swedish working-class mothers — all below thirty (Sellerberg 1975a)[2].

A specific contradiction prevails in the lives of these young mothers — children were in focus, claiming extensive spending and intensive attention, occupying the very heart of their mothers' existence. And *precisely* because of this greediness that is part and parcel of children's role in relation to their mothers, and vice versa, the mothers made very conscious attempts to maintain a boundary *against* children becoming the be-all and end-all of their lives.

In the ensuing discussion, this duality is a crucial factor. The way in which "being inside" is able to reinforce, and lend added emphasis to, "being outside" is presented as the central quality of modern motherhood awareness. These young women are almost devoured by a role — and the very awareness of this condition fosters an urge to step outside, transcending the "voracity" inherent in the role.

Hence, the restrictions of modern motherhood are presented as being upheld by the bearers of the mother's role themselves, *both* from within and from without.

From Within: Children in Focus of All Attention

Having children usually entails significant changes in an individual's way of life. A mother may have to terminate her salaried work for some time; at the same time, the expenditure of the family increases. A mother's freedom of movement will most certainly decrease, including her opportunities to go out in the evenings, etc.

Instead of forming part of her life as a whole, her spending of time and money will now be channelled into new directions.

Formerly — in the early stages of the twentieth century — most parents would have to use their money for bare necessities when spending it on their offspring. Moreover, they may have regarded spending as something which would be repaid in the future, in that they would themselves be cared for by grown-up children.

The young mothers I interviewed told me, at length, about their thoughts and plans regarding their children's toys and clothes. When they were out shopping, their children would be at the very centre of their minds. A young woman operator: "You do have a soft spot for them and give them more things than you really intended to. You are so very fond of them." The mothers stressed the large amounts of money they spent on their children.

At the same time, they emphasized the way in which the children were in the focus of moral attention. These women thought, planned, and purchased for their offspring — but their anticipation of gratitude was correspondingly intense. A mother would watch her child very closely to find out what he or she felt about the new purchase. The extent to which the child was truly grateful was a matter of careful assessment. A hospital cleaner expressed this fusion of generous giving and expectation in these terms:

"Politeness is important. . . They're so spoiled nowadays. Also, it seems they've got to have everything now. My boy has a bike worth 500 crowns. He can hardly ride a bike yet."

A supermarket cashier, wife of a bricklayer: "They appear so spoiled these days. They don't appreciate their toys the way we did." A punching operator: "They *must* show gratitude, too. They mustn't grab for themselves. When they get something they should give you something in return, shouldn't they?"

While the children were in the material focus of spending, they thus held the same position with regard to their mothers' eager moral attention. This close observation of children is something new mothers absorb from the very first; behavior, thoughts, physical symptoms etc. are constantly being interpreted. New mothers are expected to show up at child welfare clinics at fairly short intervals. Right through babyhood and childhood, mothers are expected to monitor their children.

In the interviews, mothers would be careful to emphasize that their children were very special individuals whose feelings and behavior only they, the mothers, could decode. "Very sensitive," "extremely shy," "needing very special treatment," etc. were typical expressions.

All women interviewed were mothers of preschool children. When the interviews took place, the issue of day care for working mothers had been debated fairly often in mass media. Consequently, municipal day-nurseries might be expected to be a matter of some interest to them. However, these working-class women seemed to know very little about day-nurseries.[3] Few had applied for places for their children. Mostly, the women seemed to look upon municipal day-nurseries as being of no relevance and hence of very little interest to them. Day-nurseries seemed alien places. (Interestingly enough, this impression prevailed in spite of an obvious geographical closeness. Many of the women could see that district's day-nursery from their windows.)

Some women even seemed ashamed when the topic was broached. Nobody else was supposed to assume responsibility for their child. A woman factory worker: "I have been at home all the time. You don't want to leave your child with somebody else. Haven't talked about it with anybody. You don't talk to others about those things." A seamstress working nights (so as to be able to look after her children during the day): "I haven't thought about day-nurseries. There used not to be many of them around."

On the whole, the thought of having "strangers" mind your small children and assume responsibility for them seemed to make these mothers uncomfortable. The second "established" possibility when you are not looking after your own children is a "municipal child-minder" (mostly a housewife looking after other people's children in her own flat or house, then often together with her own). She is a housewife, just like the mother herself. Still, she *is* a stranger. A punching operator:

"I don't quite trust her, though she does seem reliable. I don't know if she makes enough time for him."

The young mothers were hence very much opposed to the thought of having their children looked after by other people. If that were the case, the children would be "out of sight" and out of the center of attention, of moral anticipation, of wishes and of present-giving during a significant part of the day.

Motherhood from Without — Recognizing the Boundaries

As the preceding pages have suggested, the children were indeed at the heart of spending and of various moral demands, forming the focus of the mothers' attention. In this sense, the motherhood role is greedy, claiming the whole person (Coser 1974). The interviewed mothers said that they experienced their new way of life as restricted, but these restrictions were felt to be voluntary, wholly chosen by themselves. Babies were something you had because you had decided to have them, not something you had been given. In the 1969 Royal Committee report on current sexuality, the term "the contraceptive society" was coined as a description of modern Sweden: "According to our accounts based on our interviews, 9.7 million instances of sexual intercourse took place during one month in the early winter of 1967 in Sweden. Nine months later 8,800 children were born. In the Swedish contraceptive society, it takes 1,100 cases of sexual intercourse for one child to be born." (The 1969 Report:23)

Naturally, the motherhood of the young women concerned was by no means always perfectly planned and rationalized. However, motherhood — planned or not — did occur in this "contraceptive context." It is in this somewhat passive sense that motherhood has decidedly become an act of will.

This consciousness of having made a choice is associated both with potent psychological focusing on children and with an element of distance, "being outside" the awareness of restrictions in relation to motherhood. Almost without exception, and in the very same words, these young mothers stress their consciousness of the new boundaries.

A seamstress, mother of two, says: "Certainly you are tied down with children. You only meet people who have children themselves. Sometimes — now and again — it gets very dull indeed. But after all, you chose to have children." And a woman cutter: "We used to go out dancing quite a lot. That is impossible now. Then we could go away for the night. We realized that things would change this way, though." A children's nurse: "You do have to plan your expenses nowadays. So you have food for the whole month. Planning everything so that you have somebody to mind the children. Anyhow, she (the daughter) did become our greatest interest."

Against Devouring

Maintaining a boundary calls for the ability to be both within *and* without, regarding it from within *as well as* from without. In brief terms, the presence of both stances, or frames of mind, makes for a situation where it is possible to be sociopsychologically devoured by a greedy, expansive role while taking precautions against being entirely "gobbled up."

The spending, the attention, the demands, the dreams and wishes of the mothers focused on their children. Significantly enough, though, the modern moral of motherhood also included the maintenance of boundaries against this centrality on the part of the children: A decent mother should *also* take steps to ensure that her children don't become the be-all and end-all of her life.

Maintaining a Physical Boundary

Children, the interviewed mothers suggested, should be important in life, but not all-important. "Boundaries" should exist. What opportunities did these young working-class mothers have, then, when it came to maintaining such a boundary? Few of them had jobs or other engagements which demanded their intellectual or emotional commitment. Middle- and upper-class women often have, and in that they have a place preserved from children, too. Instead, working-class mothers had to utilize other boundaries. They fixed a boundary against the intrusion of children within the home, a demarcation in a physical sense: "No children in the living-room" was a firm principle in their rearing of their children.

Accordingly, most children were not permitted by their mothers to play in — or sometimes even to be in — the living-room, often called "the big room." A shop assistant, wife of a plumber, said:

> "They are allowed to be in their own room, in the kitchen and in the hall. They are not forbidden to be in'the big room.' But they must not run their cars on the table and things like that. When they were smaller, we put up a gate between the living-room and the hall."

A shop assistant, mother of two:

> "They aren't allowed in the big room. And they don't go there either. I have many ornaments on low tables and shelves in there. And when they are playing with hockey sticks and things like that. . . We have a colour television set, and a valve might easily crack. The furniture is robust, but you do want to have some place which is tidy, don't you?"

It may be seen as the work of irony — or rather the work of middle-class interior planners — that on this residential estate, the living-room door was, quite simply, excluded from the fittings in the apartments. In brief, there was no easily accessible instrument for demarcation. This very lack was the most common complaint which the young working-class mothers voiced in respect of their homes. A hairdresser: "I prefer them not to be in the big room. But you can't shut the door because there isn't one."

In these pages, modern motherhood has been described as a synthesis: involvement and the deliberate withholding of this very involvement. Consequently, "decent motherhood" in the view of the interviewed young women consists in bringing your children into your psychological center as well as — and at the same time as — keeping them out of that center: no children in the big room. "That's a place where Mum and Dad have their evening coffee."

Notes

1. Simmel 1971, pp. 355-356.
2. The study was conducted in the city of Malmö (about 45,000 inhabitants) in the early 70's. The women interviewed all had preschool children. 224 interviews were conducted, about half of

the mothers interviewed being working-class. Interviewing was limited to a selected housing estate in Malmö. The article (Sellerberg 1975a) is based upon the results obtained from a selected category of the sample: those mothers who were working-class and below the age of 30.

3. Studies of parental interest in day care indicate that the mothers who regard day nurseries as a matter of course tend to have a higher education (Swedish TUC survey).

2

Restrained Expressivity

*The telling and reception of stories, etc., is not an
end in itself but only means for the liveliness,
harmony, and common consciousness of the
"party." It not only provides a content in which all
can participate alike; it also is a particular
individual's gift to the group - but a gift behind
which its giver becomes invisible...[1]*

Georg Simmel on Sociability

In certain contexts, human beings become especially anxious to
express aspects of their personalities — opinions, experiences, tastes.
Life in a geriatric hospital constitutes such a context. Here, patients are
aged people who, in the course of long lives, have formed personal
views on a variety of matters. My study concerned views connected
with food (Sellerberg 1983). However, the terms of hospital existence
were contradictory — the wish to express personal features was
constantly restrained, even rejected. Hence, intensely personal things
could only be expressed in certain restrained social forms: sociable or
discreet.

Background

On Swedish geriatric wards, few patients have private rooms. Hence
patients are forced to share most of their waking and sleeping moments
with others. They have little opportunity to influence the choice of food,

the hours, hospital activities or their lives in general. Also, patients are rarely able to use personal belongings or particular foods and dishes so as to express a personal identity. The significance of this lack of personal control is reported by Rubenstein (Rubenstein 1987, pp. 225-238; Sherman and Newman 1977; Kalymun 1982). In this sense, hospitals offer strictly collective situations.

The hospital situation in Sweden is virtually the same throughout the country, as practically every institution is state-controlled. Consequently, routines, hours, even physical buildings are similar.

The interviews concerned the personal opinions of patients regarding hospital food. One might have expected to hear tales about the food at home — what dishes were served, for instance, and how delicious they were. In addition, these old residents — especially the former housewives, could have been expected to describe, in exact terms, how they used to cook and what they ate before they came to the institution. They seldom did, though.

At the same time, however, the hospital food seemed to be of great personal interest to the patients. They waited for the dining cart in groups, discussing what was about to be served. Thus, the reason for the failure of patients to voice their opinions in an unrestrained manner was not a lack of interest.

The important thing was that each personal expression had to be mooted in a restrained form. The reason for this seems to have been that presenting a personal opinion (expressing the personal) in this social context amounted to emphasizing oneself, one's own private life. Thus, when the patients voiced their opinions and spoke about the food they liked, they resorted to very particular ways of expression which might be termed the sociability and the discretion strategies (see below).

Purpose of the Study

The original purpose of this study was formulated by the hospital administration. The administrators wanted to know the patients' personal opinions about the hospital food. What points in time, what dishes were preferred? Before my qualitative interview study, other researchers had attempted to perform a questionnaire survey at the two relevant geriatric hospitals. However, very few of the patients answered. The problem is obvious: patients were unable to reply when asked for their personal views in a questionnaire listing the dishes they were served — the reason being that to most patients in this setting, personal preferences of that kind had to be given socially acceptable expression.

The patients found it difficult to state how they evaluated dishes. Questions about choices and possible alternatives to existing mealtimes — and to the dishes that were served — seemed irrelevant and incomprehensible. The data from these quantitative surveys were impossible for the administration to utilize. Hence, a new and different kind of study was decided upon.

The purpose of the study was, once again, to acquaint the administrators of the local health-care system with the preferences of patients regarding mealtimes and food. But the problem of recording personal opinions remained. Choices were not pondered by the patients. For example, one question in the qualitative study asked whether the patients thought breakfast was served at the right time in the morning. This question was misunderstood. The answer was often "No, it is served here at a fixed time." This fact is significant. The answers were concerned with the question whether the staff served the meal punctually. They never expressed personal views on the matter.[2]

The analysis of the tape-recorded discussions of patients about the hospital food showed that some points of view were accepted, listened to, followed up. Other opinions were greeted with silence. Patients around interpreted them as unacceptable and problematic utterances. The actual content of these opinions was of little significance. The sociological functions of such utterances were very different, though.

In general terms, the socially acceptable personal opinions of patients are those which can *be added to* by others. This possibility of continuation is of great importance. By means of picking up, participating, and answering at the appropriate social level, the patients on the ward could raise personal expression to the sociability level.

In the geriatric hospitals, two different forms of personal expression are discerned. *Sociability* consists in building up an interaction of personal expression, and responding to it with examples of one's own. In the form called *discretion*, people respond by overlooking the personal expression. In both cases, the personal element becomes integrated in social interaction. Fellow patients play along by adding "building blocks" in the form of their own points of view; or they pretend not to notice the personal factor.

The way in which personal views were expressed seemed to be a crucial factor in this collective environment. The patients had different solutions to this predicament. Individual preferences were formulated in specific ways in order to be accepted by the table collective. Two main forms of acceptable expressions were distinguished: the first is the more active form, in which individual statements must elicit an active collective response. This is referred to as the *sociability* form. The second form is based on *discretion* — that is to say, the passive collective response consists in not noticing.

The Sociability Forms

In the present discussion, the sociability form is exemplified by four types: vindication arguments; humorous anecdotes; stories in common; and references to what is customary. The de-emphasizing of personal traits is common to all these types of "sociable" expression (Simmel 1964, p. 53). This pattern provides a content in which all can participate alike. In this interaction, the invisibility of the one who tells a story or supplies an argument is of great importance. It is an "individual's gift to the group — but a gift behind which its giver becomes invisible" (Simmel 1964, p. 53).

Vindication Arguments

Personal views on the hospital food are sometimes expressed as statements of injustice, *vindication arguments*. The patient criticizes his or her food by speaking as the representative of a group, and by making a comparison with more favored groups. For example, one man, himself a "porridge eater," argues strongly in favor of justice for this group in comparison with the "buttermilk eaters":

> "Why can't we have porridge every morning? There is no porridge here on Mondays, Wednesdays and Fridays... And why do they bring buttermilk *every* morning to those who have that for breakfast?"

This comment immediately starts a heated discussion. The others around the table agree. His point is justified, and other injustices are brought up. Diabetics compare themselves with those who receive ordinary food. One diabetic patient states, "The others get Swiss rolls, waffles and wheat bread. But because of the rules, all I get is a dry slice of bread!"

Some patients also make comparisons with the way things used to be in the hospital. Viewpoints concerning the withdrawal of previous privileges can be continued by most of the others around the table. These vindication arguments from patients encourage further elaborations which are subsequently included in the sociability discourse.

The Humorous Anecdote

Sometimes views on the food take a *humorous* turn. Others at the table join in with their own examples.

According to Coser (1980, pp. 81-97), co-patients did not consider it acceptable to say, "I do not like that beef." The same point was, however, tolerated when phrased, "Those hamburgers today were as hard as rocks, if I'd bounced them against the wall, they'd have come right back." In the first expression, a patient put forward an individual point of view in an unacceptably self-oriented manner. In the second, the opinion invited the others around the table to contribute instances of their own.

The social functions of humor are various (Coser, 1959; Coser 1960; Coser 1980; Fine 1983; Orbdlik 1942; Pogrebin & Poole 1988; Radcliffe-Brown 1940). Its function of releasing stress, as well as the way it promotes social solidarity, has often been emphasized (Coser 1959; Coser 1960; Pogrebin & Poole 1988, p. 183).

In this study, however, a special aspect of humor is relevant. Humorous interaction, joking descriptions which elicit other joking descriptions, functions as a barrier keeping intimate personal references out. Simmel stresses this, frequently neglected, side of humorous descriptions. Hence the telling of jokes about the food, though often a mere pastime, reflects the elements of sociability. "It keeps the conversation away from individual intimacy and from all purely personal elements that cannot be adapted to sociable requirements" (Simmel 1964, p. 53).

Stories in Common

The patients' personal viewpoints about the hospital food are also expressed in the "stories in common." In the hospital environment, a very special kind of story about food acquires common interest: the type that concerns food which was served, but did not agree with medical orders. These topics attract extra response and participation in this social milieu. The others in the group feel encouraged to come up with their own examples, both stories from the realm of personal experience and tales based on hearsay.

Sometimes, the patients continue these stories by adding historical references of some length — "atrocity stories" — about food served contrary to medical instructions (Baruch 1981, pp. 275-295; Webb & Stimson 1976). Such stories function as sociability enhancers. When personal matters are presented in a particular way, more examples are invited from those sitting around. On that basis, they belong within the framework of sociability.

References to What Is Customary

Personal "food opinions" are also expressed as references to *established customs*. In these cases, the Swedish home-cooking tradition is frequently invoked. This is an objective guiding principle for food which the other patients can also securely relate to. It can take the form of arguments about what a *real* breakfast should consist of, what is a *real* dessert, or what should be served for dinner on Thursdays, according to traditional rules. One woman states her personal view on the desserts. Fresh fruit (today's dessert), she argues, is not a traditional dessert in Sweden. She is excited, and the others go along with her:

"Occasionally they have a banana for dessert. That's not worth coming here for!"
"What should it be?" I asked.
"A small baked apple, or rice pudding with apple. Or blue-berry compote."

When the point is made, the others at the table nod in agreement. Those would have been *real* desserts! They are, in other words, typical Swedish desserts — common ground, well-known to all. Patients can express personal opinions and see them securely established within the framework of sociability.

When it is Thursday, split-pea soup with pork is traditional in Swedish home-cooking. A nurse answers a patient who asks about Thursday dinner:

"You can look at the menu in the kitchen. It's sausage and mashed potatoes."

Even if personal views are taboo, the patient can — in this case — react without running a risk. All the others are as surprised as he is, and he knows they are.

"What! Not pea soup? It's *Thursday* today. . ."

On another day, a patient expresses a very strong opinion: it is wrong not to serve herring on a Tuesday, the "herring day." The conversation continues, and the yearning for herring is further legitimized by others around the table. Several people speak of the nutritional value of herring. "Herring is good for the stomach." One of the men even asserts, "The body needs herring once a week."

Within these established customary terms, a patient can even refer to something as personal as "home":

"Codfish and mustard sauce at home. It was good. I had that once a week." This reference is to the traditional and customary. It is traditional to have fish, often herring or codfish, for dinner once a week, frequently on Tuesdays. The other patients around the table agree.

The customary can, however, include other important values. One example is the housewife morale common to many of the female patients. These personal, critical views on the hospital food refer to thrift, and to the use of left-overs. The women thus often talk to one another about the wastefulness in the hospital's food service. The topic provides an air of shared understanding, expressed in personal comments: "They could add more potatoes to the meat to make it go further." The other women agree, adding the argument that the food would not have been so salty if there had been more potatoes. — "It's a pity they are so stingy with the potatoes." And so the conversation on the hospital's food waste goes on.

Autonomous Forms

Sometimes, sociable discussions around the tables seem to acquire a value of their own. Subjective expression vanishes. The same opinions trigger the same social continuations. This may go on for years. Groups of patients often keep drifting towards the same conversational subject. At one table, the saltiness of the food has been the common topic for many years. It is, in the more solemn words of Georg Simmel, a case of autonomous forms: ". . . since in sociability the concrete motives bound up with life-goals fall away" (Simmel 1971, p. 129). Actually, the degree of saltiness is of little interest. Instead, the whole thing is a matter of common ground and social participation — and of heated involvement in individual opinions without appearing personal.

The Non-Verbal Form — Discretion

Sociability invites the possibility of interpreting personal utterances as impersonal ones, using verbal expressions. But many of the geriatric patients had difficulties in expressing themselves verbally. They had speech impairments of various kinds. Still, a kind of silent sociable interaction can take place. Patients express their own opinions by putting certain foods aside, or by not eating certain meals. The group is *not* supposed to take any notice of this. The appropriate response in this interaction from the others present is silence, pretending not to see; that is, *discretion*. "For, discretion consists by no means only in the respect for the secret of the other, for his specific will to conceal this or that from us, but in staying away from the knowledge of all that the other does not expressly reveal to us" (Simmel 1964, pp. 320-321). It is a typical Simmelean paradox that the expression should reveal to the others who are present that it is a concealed one! Simmel summarizes it in the rule "what is not revealed must not be known." In a case of discretion, then, the others interact and participate by not caring about the individual expressions.

For example, one man speaks very critically of the patients he has *heard* complaining. They are the non-discreet ones. They commented loudly upon the food they did not like and left it aside. In the interview, however, it came out that he himself very regularly — without ever commenting on it — left his pastry bun at every evening meal, and that he had done so for years. Where discretion is concerned, a personal opinion of a meal is revealed in this hidden way. Certain dishes are *always* left behind. Some of the patients refrain not only from certain dishes, but also from entire meals, making other dishes or meals "theirs." A more comprehensive food strike, on the other hand, would have been a conspicuous individual expression, and possibly offensive to the norms of the ward. It is the opposite of discretion. In discretion, too, the personal expression is transformed into a collective one. The form is interactive. The "right," or appropriate, response from the other participants is indispensable.

The Rule-Breakers

But not all the patients were willing, or able, to express their personal views and wishes in these acceptable — i.e., restrained — forms. Some patients were quite psychologically rigid in their personal claims. In one of the hospitals, patients who were extremely persistent in making specific demands as regards the food or other hospital routines were actually transferred to "the isolation ward." Staff members described these patients as insensitive to their environment. "They are perhaps not so sick physically, but more psychologically. . . they are perfectionists." They were neither able to participate in sociability nor in the silent discretion.

In addition to these so-called perfectionists, some patients constantly broke the sociability or discretion rules. These rule-breakers presented their complaints in a socially offensive "me-form", for example: "I am not familiar with food like this!" These patients also compared hospital conditions with the life they had led at home. They kept bringing up their own private experiences, sometimes attempting to demonstrate that they did not belong in the ward.

One unsociable and unrestrained method of presenting a personal food opinion is the "final statement." Personal opinion is thus formulated as absolute, and no collective extension or confirmation is possible. These impermissible comments by rule-breakers are often one-sided, personal, unfavorable descriptions of the food. A woman criticizes it by saying, "You could vomit sometimes, when you see the food here." Others remain silent. They could hardly elaborate on such a final, categorical statement.

Comments from other patients indicate that patients who indulge in this type of unsociable personal outspokenness are well-known outsiders. Most patients exhibit a marked distance towards these violators of hospital etiquette. One explanation frequently offered by the other patients is that rule-breakers had probably experienced a bad home environment. Now, in hospital, they would compensate by complaining.

Some patients would actively oppose a violator, trying to demonstrate that his/her views and behavior were inconsistent. One rule-breaker patient might say that she really hated some of the hospital dishes. Those sitting around would protest, saying that in fact she ate it with gusto. "She eats everything she gets, there is no stopping her!" Thus, unsociably expressed views were made even more illegitimate.

There were also patients who transcended the norms for the discreet type. They were openly personal in a non-verbal way. Some senile patients sitting with the others around the dining tables behaved in a conspicuously personal manner. These violators are quite openly discussed by the other patients ("They're difficult. What can be done about them?"), who thus mark out a distance between themselves and the unsociable ones. A highly significant social dividing line in the geriatric wards is clearly established.

The Dividing Line

When patients mark their distance from rule-breakers, they react as members of a group which invests considerable effort in keeping itself at a certain social level. Non-rule-breakers are afraid of becoming like some intractable patients who sit around at mealtimes. The line between rule-breakers and non-rule-breakers was of great significance. Sociability and discretion were strategies employed in order to take part in, and reaffirm, one's belongingness to and integration with the people on the "right" side of the line. By resorting to these strategies, patients resisted the designations "asocial," "anti-social," "indiscreet" — and "senile."

A clear demarcation line exists between those who use the "good forms" and those who do not. Being able to express personal desires in acceptable ways in the group environment calls for a certain social sensibility. It is interesting, though, that occasionally even the rather senile patients made an effort to show such sensitivity. Patients aware that they did not master the sociability forms tried not to expose themselves. Being able to handle the acceptable forms of expression seems especially important in institutions like the ones studied here, where patients often stay for the rest of their lives. If forms are not maintained, the demarcation line separating those who go by the rules and those who break them is transgressed.

According to Prus, it is especially important to resist designations and labels when the undesired designations are likely to become permanent (Prus 1975, p. 5). In this case, it was likely that the senile identity would become an established designation. Once the people in your immediate environment have placed you in the category of those whose understanding is defective, and with whom no normal interaction is possible, it is difficult to remove this label.

When people anticipate that highly unfavorable consequences will arise from the relevant designation, they are likely to resist it, too (Prus 1975, p. 5). Interaction between patients was patent and visible to the environment, including the staff. Not to be able to behave oneself could easily become a bench-mark (Morgan 1982, p. 43). It might entail a staff decision to transfer the patient concerned to a special ward. In addition, such a failure to comply with accepted standards of behavior may lead to the patient's being pushed out of the prevailing pattern of social integration without being admitted to any other social context — in short, to loneliness. Outsiders are by definition asocial and "private" in their relationships with others.

Discussion

The two geriatric hospitals described here are of the kind in which patients normally reside for the remainder of their lives. These hospitals accommodate those individuals who are no longer able to live in a private setting, as a result of either physical or mental disability. Therefore, administrators generally felt that the individual needs of these "inmates" could not be ignored. As a staff member said: "If a person is so sick that he can hardly think of being able to go home again, then the hospital must become a home to him."

The hospital administrators tried hard to find out how the personal views of patients could be taken into account. This desire for reform demonstrates that the existence of patients' individual points of view is acknowledged. This is felt to be a social issue by those who run the hospitals in question.

Both sociability and discretion are *informal* integrative belongingness interactions. Patients respond spontaneously to one another in the forms described.

These informal interactions can be contrasted with the different food reforms initiated by the hospital administration: A "suggestion card" and a "meal card" were introduced in order to establish the personal preferences of patients. Every patient received a personal meal card. On this card were vacant areas for filling in foods that the patient was particularly fond of or perhaps did not appreciate at all. How, then, did the patients perceive these opportunities of presenting personal opinions on the food? The interviews showed that the majority of patients were totally unaware of the cards' existence.

The purpose of the so-called suggestion card was to capture the more spontaneous, personal food wishes. The patient could order his/her favorite food and have it the following day. But on most of the wards, staff told us that none of the patients utilized the suggestion card.

In brief, the reforms did not function the way they were intended to. One primary reason for this failure is probably that they were *contrary* to the two important social norms — both to the sociability and the discretion ethos. The "card reforms" were based on the myth according to which informal social life can be administered, and private expressions in collective life can be openly channeled. But any such administrative ordering of personal views easily becomes an administrative take-over.

As was pointed out above, these plans for reform demonstrate that the existence of patients' individual points of view is recognized as a social issue. In this situation, what the administration regards as successful reforms becomes a matter of particular significance. Such reforms may be used as signs to the outside world that the hospital is good at taking care of the personal lives of the patients. One reform which was proudly presented thus concerned the private alcohol consumption of patients. It has long been a sensitive question in Sweden to what extent the old people in geriatric wards and old people's homes should be allowed to drink their own alcohol. At one point, such consumption was forbidden. However, the official debate made it clear that it was felt to be wrong to deny the old patients this possibility. Both hospitals therefore had special cupboards in which bottles of liquor were stored with patients' personal name labels on them. These cupboards were proudly displayed to visiting delegations. — For various reasons, these particular personal wishes had come to be so strongly supported and respected by the administration that they were utilized for demonstration. Staff members were able to show visitors that there was room for individualism in the hospital collective.

Still, these open declarations of personal tastes are non-restrained. They are contrary to sociability and discretion norms. Making sure that the informal remains just that seems to be a precarious business.

Notes

1. Simmel 1964, p. 53.
2. Research for this study took place in two Swedish long-term health-care hospitals, specializing in the care of the elderly. Taped interviews and observations in the wards were conducted by a post-graduate student, a

registered nurse, and the author. 87 patients were interviewed while sitting around the mealtime tables. This sample comprised approximately one fourth of the total number of patients and one half of the staff members. The difference in percentage between participating patients and staff is due to difficulties in communicating with many of the patients, a large number of whom are senile.

Consequently, almost all the interviewing was performed in a group setting. The two interviewers sat with patients in the dining-rooms and sometimes with groups of eating patients in the patients' rooms. A small tape-recorder was set up in the middle of the group. The interviewer explained that she was interested in knowing what the patients thought about the food and about mealtimes, and told them that the information was to be included in a report to the administration, which hoped to serve food which was liked by the patients. The interviews took place during the day in the course of several weeks. Observational techniques used at mealtimes also allowed for the recording of non-verbal expressions.

Naturally, objections can be made against this method. The views expressed by patients in these groups are hardly likely to be truly personal, and deeply felt, opinions. In such a setting, however, collective influence could never be avoided. More important still, the ordinary life of a patient in a geriatric hospital is a group existence. Any outward expression of personal preferences has to take place in this collective setting. In view of these circumstances, a group interview seemed realistic.

Also, it could be argued that the presence of the tape-recorder affects the answers. In actual fact, I believe that the tape-recorder, though visible, is forgotten after a number of days together around meals. In any case, the Swedish Sociological Association prohibits the implementation of secret studies using hidden recorders. The subjects should always give their consent to the study.

Of course, the method outlined above is of particular importance with regard to the "anti-personal-account" results of the study. Most of the interviewing was done *in groups* of four to six patients.

3

Superordination from Subordination

*It has been possible, at least in many cases, to show the sociologically decisive **reciprocal effectiveness**, which was concealed under the one-sided character of influence and being-influenced.*

Georg Simmel on Superordination.

The following quotation, which describes the situation in public houses during the early years of the twentieth century, was taken from a historical work on the trade union of the catering occupations.

In working-class newspapers, much has been written about the working conditions of waitresses. Since a partly new legislation on restrictions came into force for the so-called "bolagskrogarna" (public houses nearly exclusively frequented by working-class people), the waitresses have become the objects of a quite specific attention. On consuming one sandwich at 10 "öre", a thirsty guest could get one dram. The desired nectar was, however, restricted to a certain number of centilitres, and it was the responsibility of the waitresses to see to it that the valid restrictions were held sacred. (Lantz 1968, p. 104)

From the same source, a published letter to the editor (from 1900) is quoted:

It is a sad experience to enter a "bolagskrog" and listen to the discontent which now prevails here. "He got one a short while ago!" "He comes from the dining room, give him nothing!" and so on. In this way, the waitresses are allowed to rule without the customer being permitted to have his say. Some flare up, and so the police are sent for and the person concerned is arrested. (Lantz 1968, p. 104)

At this time, a new set of laws prescribed that waitresses assume a superordinate role, keeping guests under control. Up to now, the staff serving at table had nearly always been male; it is interesting to see that the male/female pattern in this occupation began to change at this time.

This illustration of the exercise of control was chosen as an introductory example for the simple reason that women's work has commonly been designated as subordinate. A very large number of studies have described the situation of women on the labor market, and the conclusion tends to be the same throughout: Women assume various kinds of subordinate positions.

By contrast, this analysis will deal with typical contradictory features in the service jobs done by women, focusing on conditions that entail subordination *and* superordination. The working conditions in some highly characteristic women's jobs are analyzed. The relevant occupations are of some quantitative importance in the sense that women form a great majority: shop assistants, waitresses and telephone operators.

Naturally, the reasoning put forward here has an underlying hypothesis: I assume that it is the presence of various contradictions in the practice of women's service jobs that makes them into jobs for women (Sellerberg 1973, 1975b). Consequently, I do not regard the actual content of the relevant work (for instance, its being concerned with such a typically "female" field of work as food) as the reason why it has become an occupation mainly for women. Nor do I believe that the element of subordination, of "serving," explains why an occupation has become characteristically "female." Instead, I regard contradictions as being, in different periods and social contexts, an element typical of women's jobs: Functioning as a controller from above is one thing; controlling from above on the basis of a subordinate position is a very different one. Assuming practical, everyday responsibility and seeming to be in charge of operations is a clear-cut position, but the entire significance of such a position changes when the person concerned is actually subordinate in the organization. In such a case, the issue of responsibility is a contradictory one; we are dealing with a situation where a person serves, practically and concretely, as a representative but does not in fact have a solid foundation to stand on.

Subordinate Superordinates

The waitresses who were supposed to serve humbly while checking what the guest ate and drank form a very obvious example of this contradiction. Actually, it can be found in a multitude of historical descriptions of the waiting-at-table occupation from different periods in time. Several decades later, in an occupational dictionary published by the National Labor Market Board, we can find the following characteristics claimed for catering professionals:

> These occupations are of a marked "service" type, and personal conduct is of the utmost importance. A polite and obliging manner and — *whenever necessary* — *a certain firmness* are essential together with a good memory for faces. (*Svenskt Yrkeslexikon* 1965, part 2, p. 228) [My italics]

In a staff-magazine article describing the working environment in Railway Restaurants, the waitress's relation to her customers is depicted in the following terms:

> Never have I seen so few and so tender young women so calm and collected when ignoring foul language and invective. . . With supreme pliability, they got drunken customers in order, removing those who fell asleep blind drunk, arms on tables. Actually there were only two difficult ones, but there could have been more if the girls hadn't been so diplomatic. — Annica, 17, and Eva, 19. (*Trumpeten* 3, 1966, pp. 8-9)

In due course, waitresses are gradually turned into barmaids. In fact, this development reinforces the element of contradiction. On the one hand, the subordination of the cafeteria assistant to the guest is regulated in "the code of service" : "The customer is always right. "The employee is subordinate to the outsider in this general sense: "Never assume a lofty air towards the customer." On the other hand, in the relation between employee and guest/customer, certain working duties also call for unambiguous control. Cafeteria assistants control payments and queuing by guests. In this technical or practical sense, the employee is superordinated to the cafeteria guests or store customers. Cashiers control the payments of supermarket visitors, initiating action among queuing customers by demanding, "Who's next?"

It is easy to see that a superordinate action gains special significance when undertaken "from below." It produces a particular reciprocity. It is typical of this kind of interaction that the person subjected to a controlling measure reacts and wants to indicate and allude to the element of subordination. In other words, there is a desire to undermine technical/practical superordination. It seems as if customers/guests, on their part, resort to certain tactics in handling this evident superordination on the part of a subordinated member of the serving staff. They use specific measures in order to undercut the superordination of the employee, e.g. indiscretion and antagonism towards the employee. Accordingly, the capability of handling indiscretion is represented as a specific occupational skill among waitresses. One waitress whose observations were included in the trade-union history quoted above said:

> Of course, I found it a bit unusual in the beginning. The customers in the public house spoke in their own specific language, which sometimes made you both shy and surprised. But it was not many days before you understood that you couldn't take everything literally... The waitress who hasn't learnt to understand the guests and reduce the racy words to the value suited to the context is to be pitied. She has chosen the wrong career in life. (Ekendahl 1942, pp. 23-24)

A literary example of this occupational experience of customers' indiscretion is given in the novel "Kungsgatan" by Ivar Lo-Johansson.

> On days when the café — which was also an eating-house because of the beer — had hot leg of pork on the stained menu card, at least twenty customers ordered leg "in heat". They pinched her affectionately when she served the food. Is this the ham "in heat"? Martha laughed and took it all in good part.
> — You, like me, would find knackwurst better, wouldn't you?
> Martha didn't show that she had heard the same joke a moment ago.
> — You can have that another time, she answered, surprisingly daring even for one of the bold ones.
> — Can I?
> (Lo-Johansson 1966, p. 115)

Changes in working duties and in the organization of the work of shop assistants seem to have subordinated the customer to the employee in a similar, technical fashion. The suave salesman of a bygone age turned into the supermarket cashier. Customers queue up in front of her, waiting their turn. As was suggested above, the relation between employee and customers is characterized by the same kinds of contradiction: The employee — a cafeteria assistant, a supermarket cashier, etc. — is controlling and initiating the actions of customers while herself remaining in a generally subordinate position.

Responsibility without Influence

Vilhelm Aubert described contradictions in the occupational role of the housemaid. The working conditions of the housemaid encouraged her to wish for avenues of satisfaction which other elements in her role denied her (Aubert 1963, pp. 414-415). Within the service organization, too (in the case of the housemaid, the employer family) the double forces of responsibility without influence — what Aubert termed displaced motivation — can be discerned.

Today, the staff waiting at table has, by and large, been transformed into cafeteria assistants. Most shop assistants have become supermarket cashiers. These groups often form quantitatively extensive, homogeneous and subordinated categories within the service organizations. The relation between, for instance, an assistant in a cafeteria belonging to a "chain" and her organization superiors — ultimately the chain management — is mostly an anonymous one.

All the same, direct contacts with every customer/guest are inescapable, and in every one of them somebody has to assume the practical responsiblity for the functioning of the service organization in day-to-day matters. In managing her working duties, the cafeteria assistant or store cashier becomes the representative of the service organization as a whole to guests/customers. These employees are often the only organizational representatives present who assume a kind of superordinate responsibility — while staying in a subordinate position.

To illustrate this contradictory pattern of responsibility from below, a staff magazine will be quoted. "The Trumpet" is a magazine for employees at the Swedish Railway Restaurants (it was quoted above). In one issue, a consultant advised restaurant-car assistants on how to handle matters of day-to-day responsibility: "Don't blame anybody else in your business. That would be of no interest to the customer." (*Trumpeten* 1, 1971, p.11)

In the same magazine, the following interview is utilized to instruct personnel:

> — What do you do when the guest complains about the food?
> — Suggest serving a new dish.
> — What do you do if the guest complains about the coffee?
> — Make fresh coffee. And if the guest still is not satisfied,
> he doesn't have to pay for it.
> — What do you do when the guest complains about the service?
> — I try as hard as I possibly can to suit the service to his wishes.

— What do you do when the guest complains about the prices?
— I try to explain the economic policy of RR as well as I possibly can. I explain to the guest that the train restaurants have to cope with much greater costs than an ordinary restaurant. I also inform him that he may write to RR and obtain any further particulars he may desire.
— What do you do when the guest is complaining about the company?
— If I can possibly answer anything, I do. Otherwise, I refer to the possibility of writing to RR for any information the customer may wish to possess.
(*Trumpeten* 1, 1971, p. 11)

In assuming the practical responsibility for business matters, these employees — the barmaid and supermarket cashier — are assuming the role of company representatives, identifying with the business. However, at the same time, the working conditions of a cafeteria assistant or a supermarket cashier entail a position very similar to that of the housemaid described by Aubert (Aubert 1963, pp. 414-415). On the one hand, working duties consist of representing the organization in matters of responsibility, a condition for involvement with the present service business. On the other hand, their subordinate position, isolated from organizational superiors, and their anonymous and restricted contacts with business superiors imply a rejection and discrediting of this specific involvement. In other words, a recurrent displacement of motivation prevails.

This state of affairs seems to me to involve a typical reciprocity, a frequent response in this contradictory situation, too. Displacement of motivation gives rise to a particular work pattern: The people concerned change jobs. In work that entails assuming responsibility of the kind outlined above, the employee's response appears to be mobility, often horizontal mobility. This was once the case with the large housemaid group. The maids would change mistresses; the change itself was felt to be important, even if the new employer/mistress was rather similar to the former one. Occupational mobility was great.

Concluding Discussion

The analyses put forward in this study are based on Simmel's specific understanding of the nature of social relations: they are dialectical, that is, they consist of opposing tendencies. They often tend to prevent each other's realization, or they tend, rather, to induce a kind of paralysis: In one case the contradictory forces reinforce each other; in another, they "clarify" each other. The waitress's control of the guest's liquor consumption gains its particular contradictory significance from being practised by a subordinate. The cafeteria assistant giving orders to customers triggers reactions precisely because she does so from a subordinate position.

So far, the aim of the present discussion has been to distinguish certain sociological formal features assumed to be common to women's service work (here: women's work in a quantitative sense). Is it possible to arrive at a reasonably precise association of the patently contradictory formal qualities with quantitative changes in the proportion of men and women who work in the relevant occupation, i.e. the sexual composition? Obviously, conclusions must be tentative.

Let us, however, start with the simultaneous sub-/superordination of the female service worker in relation to customers/guests. The Swedish restaurant business has long been characterized by various social controls, e.g. liquor-restriction laws. A comparison seems to indicate that nations distinguished by some kind of restrictive legislation do tend to have a higher percentage of "women waiters". Moreover, in the case of Sweden the sexual composition in the occupation seems to have begun to change in connection with the introduction of this legislation.

Organizational changes (like the self-service system, valid both for cafeteria assistants and shop assistants) also entailed a technical superordination for the employee. This change seems to have been accompanied by a marked alteration in the occupational sexual composition, too. As it was being implemented, men began to disappear from these occupations in large numbers.

Seen from this angle, the working conditions of telephone operators acquire significant analytical importance, too. In managing their tasks (connecting subscribers, making them wait for their turn, etc.), telephone operators are — in this limited sense — very clearly in control of customers. The highly technical prerequisites of the operator's job invest her with this specific type of initiative, and hence with superordination. At the same time, the telephone operator's work is very patently a service job, the code of service safeguarding the general superordination of customers. The particular opposing tendencies adumbrated in this chapter, sub-/superordination associated with modern, and "female," service jobs, are highly prevalent in the operator occupation. It might be added that in Sweden, this occupation has been, and still is, the exclusive province (100 per cent) of women.

4

Trust

*Modern life is a "credit economy" in a much
broader sense than a strictly economic one.*
Georg Simmel on Truthfulness and Lying

In the modern world, the phenomenon of trust is often thought of as a kind of remnant from an earlier, community-type society. This is a misleading notion, though. Modern trust is different from traditional trust.

An essential feature in the ensuing line of argumentation is that trust is always an ongoing process. It can never be a remainder or a survival. It must be taken care of on a continuous basis, and it has to be socially nurtured. The reason for the importance of continuity is that trust — ancient or modern — may, at any moment, be reinforced or destroyed by new information. In our more mobile — and messier — information society, trust is a more vulnerable and volatile thing than it used to be. On the other hand, these conditions also facilitate the reinforcement of trust.

Traditional Boundary-Building Trust

In village life, trust was based on personal information. Trust was circumscribing. As Aubert writes, "The population trusted their kin, neighbors and a few figures of authority. However, there were few social bonds capable of creating a basis for trust *beyond* this limited circle" (Aubert 1976, p. 3). Consequently, distrust was quite simply used against outsiders. The boundaries of the village, gaps in class position, race, etc., constituted normal closures. Trust was constricting and boundary-building in character.

For instance, a retailer and his customer would usually know — or, at least, know about — each other. Mutual information was frequently extensive and tended to remain stable. Trading outside the boundaries of established trust seemed unethical. This pattern still exists in the countryside among the old people there, as transpired from a survey concerning consumer behavior where I taped a number of interviews with older farm-laborers concerning their shopping behavior (Sellerberg 1976). One of them, for example, informed me that he had *had to* change the shop where he bought his clothes. First, he had personally known the owners of the store. Then everything was changed, as a new owner took over the shop:

"These old chaps who had the place before were really fantastic. . . I'd joke with them and they'd joke with me and I'd have a good time. But then the store was sold to some fellow called Svensson. He got new sales staff and revamped the shop and everything, so that when you went in you could hardly recognize where you were. It wasn't the same any more, so *I was forced to change,* you see."

This farm-worker saw no alternative but to change to another store. There he *knew* something about the person with whom he would have to do business. "I know the fellow who owns this shop. He's Sven Karlsson. He was born in a town not far from here. That's my reason for going to him. He's well-known here and well-liked in every way" (See Sellerberg 1976, p. 96.). The interviewee also knew that the father of this particular shop-keeper was "a decent guy".

Another ex-farm-laborer described the special trust between him and his day-to-day grocer. He could do his shopping even when he had left his money at home. And for his own part, he returned the money if he had been given too much change . . .

"It doesn't make any difference if I want to buy for ten or a hundred crowns and have forgotten my money at home. 'You can pay me next time', and so they make a note in the accounts. . . It's a nice feeling that they've got confidence in you and that you can buy what you want. The reason is you're well-known. So they trust you and know that you're reliable. Of course you couldn't get any credit if you went to a place where they didn't know you. . ."

Another farm-hand, 65 years old, describes a distrusted trader, a peddler he knew nothing about. As was pointed out above, traditional trust is circumscribing:

"He came here last year. He was a gypsy. That I could see. He had a little Opel and sold some brushes and other junk. 'No,' I said, 'if I want a brush I'll buy it at the local shop here.' I told him to go to hell. And he hasn't been here since."

His reactions were quite different toward another peddler. This trader quickly introduced himself — "an ex-policeman, well known to all the others here":

"A car stopped here a week ago. I went out and greeted the man. He said, 'You know about the clothes-dealer from Storboda, don't you?' But I'd never heard of him. 'But I've been here lots of times,' he said, 'and I've been to your neighbors. . .' So we started talking. He'd got a big clothes store in Storboda. . . And we stood there talking. . . And so I bought some stockings and shirts and. . . He had fine stuff. I didn't get anything cheaper from him, that's true. But he was a nice guy, regular and honest. He'd been a policeman in x-town. But he'd got a heart condition and had had to leave that job. Still, he was a decent sort. In this case there was no harm in buying."

In the circumstances recounted above, boundary maintenance was an unambiguous rationale of trust. Ever more precise intersections could be drawn by means of these boundaries: The most trusted, the not-so-much trusted, and — quite often — those people who were very well known to be untrustworthy. A retailer who sold poor-quality merchandise was labelled a "swindler" on the local grapevine. In the countryside, a furniture dealer described in the interviews was forced to leave the area. The townspeople said that he had cheated too much over his second-hand transactions. — An elderly man commented, "He cheated a lot of people before. He was forced to leave. He was taking too much money.

But people just stopped paying for what they had bought, so they had to come and take it back." His opportunities of doing local business became quite limited. Still, he could trade with people from outside the local area.

Opportunity Makes the Trust

These observations might serve as a basis for discussing the characteristics of modern urban trust. Now, the rationale of trust is no longer made up of boundaries that exclude something extraneous and unreliable.

Niklas Luhmann has inquired into the new possible rationales of trust, speculating, "It is too obvious that the social order does not stand and fall by the few people one knows and trusts. There must be other ways of building up trust which do not depend on the personal element. But what are they?" (Luhmann 1979, p. 46).

Simmel stressed that modern trust must, in various ways, function so as to open up boundaries. In that way, trust becomes especially important, particularly in modern society. "Our modern life is based to a much larger extent than is usually realized upon the faith in the honesty of the other. . . We base our gravest decisions on a complex system of conceptions, most of which presuppose the confidence that we will not be betrayed" (Simmel 1964, p. 313).

Simmel emphasizes the great importance of what he terms objective knowledge/information to present-day trust, arguing that "confidence no longer needs any properly personal knowledge." - - - "The objectification of culture has decisively differentiated the quanta of knowledge and ignorance necessary for confidence."

A number of new developments in modern retailing — the new consumer legislation, new and more intricate systems of product comparison (price, weight, contents, etc.), the self-service system — constitute this process of objectification.

These are "external facts," to quote Simmel's phrase (Simmel 1964, p. 319). The change in the type of information from personal to so-called external facts could certainly be described as a case of "the objectification of culture."

However, it is important not to over-emphasize such external facts as consumer legislation, declaration of contents, etc., as necessary trust components. Instead, they could be seen as means of creating openings in any local limitations of the kind described above. Actually, trust may evolve against a background of dishonesty — and expire in the regulated consumer-guaranteed contexts.

One example is the "caveat emptor" trade. It is not rare for "ordinary citizens" to become parties in black-market or "shady" transactions. In a study of "fencing," a criminal talking about selling stolen goods showed a certain contempt for these "decent" customers:

> You meet people in cafés and so on. . . and they talk. When you think about it, people are pretty cheeky. They look at you and they know who you are. I got to know some people in the house where I lived. When I moved out, I knew that Nilsson on the third floor needed new winter tyres. I could make SEK400 out of such a deal. He'd get them with studs and everything. And the next morning there's a Volvo on the other side of town without any wheels. Instead Nilsson puts the new ones on his car. . . and then there's Nilsson's birthday. His son knows who I am. . . so there's a colour TV. And they talk with others and so forth. So the stolen things seldom stay with us. They pass out into regular society. . . (Persson 1977, pp. 51-53)

Obviously, this trade generated its own trust. The price is "a special treat for you" — and the transaction is anonymous. — Weber assumed that any trade transaction called for trust in order to come into existence (Weber 1968b, p. 884). But it may be the other way around. Elements in the trade interaction develop trust for this special occasion.

This part of the discussion was headed "opportunity makes the trust," a travesty of the saying according to which 'opportunity makes the thief." It lays stress on the necessarily mobile, flexible aspect of modern trust.

The Importance of Uncertainty

Simmel — and others — have thus maintained that traditional trust relations were based on personal information whereas modern ones rely on objective, external facts. But things do not appear to be that simple.

Simmel feels that the vitality of trust is strengthened in the urban society. A vast quantity of external facts make anonymous relations into possible trust relations. They open up boundaries, creating options. However, I do not believe that they engender trust.

In descriptions of Swedish consumer legislation, progressive achievement is stressed, and commentators praise the security of the consumer whose knowledge about regulations and laws is up-to-date. Even so, consumer legislation appears to strive for the impossible, that is to secure trust.

Trust always emerges at an intermediate stage between knowledge and ignorance about the other party (See Simmel, 1964, p. 318). Someone who knows everything does not need to trust. To be able to feel trust, on the other hand, it is necessary to know at least something.

Consequently, we must to possess both knowledge and ignorance. Knowledge alone cannot create trust. The synthetic rationale of trust in our modern society gains importance in situations involving risks, as it is the combined existence of knowledge and ignorance that has the potential of creating trust.

Clearly, then, I feel that trust necessarily embodies uncertainty. Hence, a very obvious striving for the totally guaranteed may lead to complications in a trust relation: Every effort towards the totally guaranteed situation will, in reality, weaken trust. A customer who actually uses his/her formal rights and controls the weight of a purchase at the special "customer scales" (which the law says should be found in every shop) takes a risk. In an interview, a person who availed himself of this opportunity, and this right, was described as the prime focus of gossip in his surroundings. "It isn't even as if he was poor or anything!"

The essence of modern trust, it seems to me, is that it will always be redirecting itself its its needs of information. The information that elicits trust in one social situation can never be guaranteed to do so in another. After all, if information could be used with absolute certainty, it could also be used deliberately, and any deliberate planning works against trust. Trust must be a precarious process: "I would never control the weight of a sack of potatoes. Never!"

All questioning becomes problematic. In situations where one of two parties wishes to obtain extra information, this must be collected in a discreet way (unless, of course, the collection of information is used for quite a different purpose, for example as a warning: "We don't really trust you"). The possible distrust inspired in these situations must be neutralized. Thus, side by side with indiscreet electronic equipment geared to watching over customers, there are special instructions and courses aimed at teaching employees how to mollify customers by means of personal comments.

It should also be noted that any deliberate signal intended to create trust may easily produce distrust. You might open your wallet and let your golden American Express card show. The salesman knows that someone who has acquired such a card is well off, and he is hence able to place more confidence in such a person. But is the card really yours, and is it not displayed in a too ostentatious manner? Trust is extra-sensitive and particularly vulnerable to precisely that which is very consciously designed.

The fact that trust cannot be planned and safeguarded often results in information turning into a by-product. Henslin, as part of an investigation, worked nights as a taxi-driver in a large city. Some data became central clues for him in judging customers: From what type of area did the customer order the car? To what type of community did he/she want to go? Did the customer sit with his/her face hidden? The time of day or night, the sex of the customer, and his or her age were also data involved in this evaluation process (See Henslin 1968, pp. 140-152). A particular type of "metropolitan" trust information is developing: Everyday topics of conversation are used as clues — which TV programs has the person seen? The weather? Vacation plans? Casual, everyday signals gain decisive importance.

Conclusion

Hence, a primary rationale of modern trust is found in the way it may evolve on the basis of sheer opportunity; the situation could engender its own trust.

A secondary rationale of modern trust is made up of the fact that it cannot possibly be safeguarded and controlled — such a possibility might lead to very deliberate utilization.

The circumstance that modern trust does not have to rest on a solid basis of familiar fact makes for a widening of potentialities which is both practical and instrumental in the mobile, changeable society of our time. Opportunity supplies information, and trust must always entail hazards and insecurity, or it might be controlled and abused. In this way, trust in our time becomes a highly flexible and exceedingly sensitive synthetic force in society, quite different from the boundary-building kind of trust which rejected everything from outside as "unreliable."

5

Two Languages of Consumption

Thus fashion on the one hand signifies union with those in the same class, the uniformity of a circle characterized by it, and, uno acu, the exclusion of all other groups.

. . .

Fashion always occupies the dividing-line between the past and the future...

Georg Simmel on Fashion

In its vicissitudes, fashion distinguishes one social stratum from another and, at the same time, one occasion from another.

I feel, however, that the social functions of fashion are not the sole point at issue here. Actually, Simmel appears to be presenting two dissimilar, and quite fundamental, rationales for the consumption of goods in general. By consuming in a certain way, the individual may show his "belongingness" to a certain group — and, in doing so, mark his distance from other groups.

By means of consumption, too, you can emphasize the contrast between situations — "yesterday" versus now, festive occasions versus everyday life, leisure versus work. Relaxing in front of the television set means that "TV slippers," in contrast to shoes, become important. On one's bicycle pedalling towards the city center, the special bike-to-town-shirt has exactly the right "feel," whereas the gardening shirt would have been quite out of place.

In the present study, the first rationale is referred to as the *group function* whereas the second is called the *contrast function*. In the course of interview studies, I found signs that these two rationales are characteristic of different social classes. The *group function* imparts special significance to middle-class consumption. Conversely, the *contrast function* is of particular importance in working-class groups. In practice, these two rationales came to function as two distinct modes of expression, two different "languages," which manifested themselves with the aid of consumption. Indeed, they were voiced and comprehensible within different social classes. The *group function* language was spoken in middle-class groups. The *contrast function* was a language of consumption that could be understood among members of the working class.

The Indices of the Two Rationales

The fact that social classes differ in matters of taste is, of course, anything but a novelty. They choose different styles of dress; and dissimilar styles prevail in their homes, too. Such differences were apparent in an interview investigation of the consumption habits of Swedes which I performed in the mid-1970s (Sellerberg 1975a; Sellerberg 1976a; Sellerberg 1976b; Sellerberg 1977).

However, I found that the dissimilarities did not involve taste alone. As was suggested above, consumption contributed to the creation of different types of linguistic usage. I would, for instance, ask such questions as, "Do you believe that many others in the neighborhood have the same taste as yourself?," "Is it important to have a personal style in clothes?," "Do you check what the other people who are going to the same party will be wearing before you make your own choice?" Young girls were also asked if they were saving for a trousseau.

The answers to these questions yielded important distinctions. My basic conception of the different rationales prevailing in the middle class and in the working class grew out of the answers to this particular type of questions.[1]

Various 'Consumption Conversations' within the Social Classes

"I should think there's something that suits every particular person best," was a reply offered by a single secretary, aged 47, living in a big city. The interview question to which she responded was, "Would you say that you've got a certain style that's typical of you, that is to say, a certain kind of clothes you tend to buy — or would you say that's not the case?"

Conversely, working-class girls often showed great surprise at the question. "Why. . . a typical personal style?" They could not quite grasp the question. *That* particular social function of dressing seemed of little importance to them.

Proportion of interviewees who claimed to have a style of their own (Percentage).

Single female city dwellers, middle class (40-47 years),	92
Young girls, upper middle class (16-18 years),	73
Young girls, working class (16-18 years),	22

Inter-group differences are considerable. Virtually all the single women in cities claimed to have a "style of their own." So did a significant majority of upper-middle-class girls. This view was not common among working-class girls, though.

When interpreting the investigation results it would, of course, be perfectly possible to proceed from the assumption that "everyone *wants* to have a personal style of dress." Some feel that they have succeeded in this respect, others do not, and here the groups differ. Such a view would presuppose that the groups speak the same "consumption language." That, however, would seem to be an erroneous assumption; it is possible to proceed further from this difference with regard to "personal style."

It seems as if something else was important in the working-class groups. Here, emphasis tended to be given to the importance of having new — and above all *different* — clothes for certain eminent social occasions, such as New Year's Eve, Easter, the Midsummer Dance, etc. The interviewees stressed the importance of having suitable clothes for the Friday dance, another outfit next Friday and never the same for both Friday and Saturday.

By means of consumption, they established contrasting situations, "yesterday" versus now, festive occasions versus everyday life, leisure versus work. TV slippers contrasted with shoes at the office and a special bike-to-town-shirt contrasted with the gardening shirt.

One working-class girl said:

"If I go out dancing on a Friday. . . then I'd *never* wear the same long trousers or blouse if I go dancing the next Friday. Never! It has to be at least three weeks or one month before I put it on again. I would have felt dirty if I had worn the same thing. Even if I washed it. . ."

"I might perhaps wear the same skirt. But *never* the same top!", says another.

"Usually, I buy something new for Midsummer Eve, New Year's Eve, and such occasions... And I get a new outfit in spring, too."

"On Midsummer Eve, those sort of days, I feel it's a must. *I've just got to wear something new!* I couldn't put on things I've worn to dances and parties before". (Child-care trainee, aged 17)

A working-class girl in her late teens said she "felt shabby" if she wore the same garment several Saturdays running. In her group, emphasizing a personal style was not a priority, nor was signalling "similarity" to the group. Instead, emphasis is placed on the situation. The clothes for special occasions must not be too ordinary, too run-of-the-mill. If they were, they would not fulfill the function of stressing the "novelty" of the situation.

In the course of the interviews, working-class girls criticized people who failed to dress suitably for a particular occasion, thereby neglecting to mark the specific character of a situation such as 'going out dancing', "going to town," "visiting the supermarket." The nature of the occasion should be indicated in one's way of dressing. "If you don't dress properly. . . you shouldn't go there, should you?" Maybe those who were criticized for their failure to dress to match the situation had a different idiom when consumption was concerned?

Other indications suggesting that there is such a thing as a "language of consumption" could be seen in the fact that members of the working class claimed to tire of their clothes more quickly than others:

The proportion of interviewees who wholeheartedly agreed with the statement "I often tire of my clothes before they're worn out" (Percentage).

Young housewives, in towns, working class (18-30 years),	44
Young girls, working class (16-18 years),	35
Young girls, upper middle class (16-18 years),	19
Single women in cities, middle class (40-47 years),	14

More than any others, it is the young working-class housewives and the young girls belonging to the working class who admit to tiring of their clothes. In those groups where it is important for clothes to mark contrasts, a stronger need for variety makes itself felt. At a certain point in time, the clothes that once signalled "now" will symbolize yesterday. It is easy to find examples of contrasts reflected by consumption in the interview replies of the working-class groups.

In the middle and upper classes, I found, it was important to express one's "belongingness" with the aid of consumption. Still, this idiom, or mode of expression, could be subtle enough: How could an individualized style in clothing among middle-class girls be a symptom of the wish to indicate belongingness to the group? Generally speaking, though, direct allusions expressed in the interviews to the taste of the "own" group did tend to be indirect. They are seldom outspoken; it is rare for someone to say "I have the same taste as many people I know." This was, in fact, the ultimate point at issue: registering the taste of the "own" group and joining in conversation with it.

Even so, it must be stated clearly that stressing one's own style — a style which is alike in different contexts — is invariably opposed to the rationale of contrast: You cannot change the way you dress in accordance with quite different social situations and accentuate the importance of your style at the same time. You show that you do not belong to the working class. But what about group taste?

In reality, it seemed as if this accentuating of an individualized style was not, first and foremost, a matter of personality. When the various personal styles were reproduced more precisely, they turned out to be pretty similar. In the interviews, the individualized dressing styles— when more closely described — were often representations of the common style of a group. By claiming a "personal style," the middle-class girl seems to represent the particular style of her own social circle.

Middle-class women were not keen on shopping for "proper things" in ordinary off-the-peg shops. Another notable circumstance was that upper- and middle-class women were more likely to agree in advance on what they deemed suitable in the way of dressing for a party. This is a significant point; it shows what might appear to be a paradoxical result: the great importance of the group — especially for those upper-class women who stressed that they had "a style of their own"!

One upper middle-class girl described white-tie parties, black-tie parties, jeans parties, scruffy "motor-club parties," etc. In this way, her social circle agreed in advance on what was to be worn. Here, consumption is given a social impetus: a kind of conversation, or dialogue, develops;

people represent and confirm the taste of their group.

> "Nowadays there are more `jeans parties'. In the beginning we had white-tie parties and informal-dress parties. That was two years ago. Lately, we've been having parties where it is pointed out that you should wear jeans... Or we may dress to match a particular film which we have all seen, such as Hot Rod Teenager."

In other words, the choice of dress expresses a sense of being part of one's own group as well as — and along with — the distance to others that is so vital.

There are other indications of this assumed sensitiveness shown towards the group. So far, the analysis has been restricted to the consumption of clothes. But the interviews also concerned other kinds of consumption. The "pro- and anti-dowry cases" are examples. Which girls were at the moment collecting "best china" or/and cutlery for their future homes? — The difference between the two groups of young girls was telling.

Percentage collecting sets of china for a future home.

Young working-class girls (16-18 years),	55
Young upper-class girls (16-18 years),	29

It is also important to note that many a middle-class girl reacted with extreme antipathy to the very thought of "china collecting."' To hell with it!' Another of these girls made the following comment on the "collector's items" she had sometimes received as presents from elderly relatives, such as grandmothers:

> "Never! Not on my life. No — and how sad I get when I receive those things. Then it is *they* who make up *my* future. And they have no right whatsoever to do that. They give something to me which I am supposed to use after my marriage and I really think that's absurd."

Comments from working-class girls were very different. To take an example: One young working-class girl (child-care trainee, aged 17) presented the following account of what she had already collected, distinguishing between "best" and "everyday" things:

"I've got to have ordinary china too, you know. For now we're saving up for a really grand set, and you can't use that every day. Same thing with cutlery - there have to be everyday knives and forks and a set of really nice ones."

Another young woman, also a child-care trainee (16 years old), had a "trousseau chest" full of towels, china, etc. Still, the purpose was not so much "bridal use" as the prospect of having her own things when moving to a flat of her own.

"Mum and Dad are giving us pieces of really fancy china, you know the sort of thing you use when giving grand parties. Then I'll go on buying a set and other things. I'm going to have the entire Sea-gull set of china, and an ordinary set for every day as well." (Child-care trainee, aged 17)

One working-class woman (aged 35), when interviewed, expressed her regrets at not being given a set of china on her marriage. She had been, and was, short of money; but she had always dreamt of a beautiful coffee-set. "I bought the stuff I needed, you know. But I always wanted one of those coffee-sets."

One working-class girl said she collected "a certain kind of cups." "It's good because people always know something for birthdays and that," was her comment.

Conversely, an upper-middle class girl said, "I've had coffee cups of Danish china given to me as presents. I'd never dare to use them. I get *terribly* upset when people give me things like that..."

Acquiring one set of china for great occasions and one for everyday use as quickly as possible enables the person concerned to mark important contrasts: between special occasions and ordinary life. One might, however, wonder why so many of the upper- and middle-class girls reacted so very unfavorably whenever china and cutlery collecting was mentioned. I believe their reaction might be explained by the opposition between china-set collecting and the "group function." In these groups, the boundary between "grand" and "ordinary" is not the point at issue. Instead — as Burns writes — it is a matter of ensuring that one's wallpaper, china, furniture, and records match those of friends in one's group (Burns, 1966, p. 321). Collection embodies a sizeable risk of acquiring models which later turn out to be "wrong" in this perspective.

"Being given such things only makes me sad." Timeless, pure white sets of china are held to be particularly beautiful by members of this group; that could have something to do with their being "safe" in respect of the group function.

Clothes help to mark the contrast between party-mood Saturday dances and everyday work, just as this week's Saturday dance is made to be different from last week's. Naturally, though, more long-term contrasts could be expressed along similar lines, "I was poor in those days — but now I'm doing fine." (An elderly person is required for such a long-term perspective.)

"No doubt about it, I've been crazy about clothes. Both the actual garments and shoes. These days, I stick to young people's stuff. /—/ No old-man cardigans and that sort of thing. Of course, many people have taken the mickey out of me about my buying that kind of clothes, but I'm not a bit bothered about what other people think. I dress the way I like..."

The man quoted here is in his seventies. He had an extremely impecunious childhood in a farm-laborer's cottage. His own interpretation is that "a man has to live some time." If you spent long periods of your life doing without things, it is natural for clothes and other material goods to acquire special importance when you finally do possess real means.

"Where fashion is concerned, I've been among the first. I suppose it's got something to do with my background. My family was very poor, and I had several brothers and sisters. Clothes were handed down, mended, patched, and worn again. Looking at my brothers, I see the same thing - once we were able to buy things ourselves, we had to have the lot. There was never any money for things when we were young, so we had to make up for it later. There were twelve of us. I can't think how they could keep us all on three hundred crowns a year. My old man was a farm-laborer... so perhaps I did indulge myself a bit, with clothes and that, when I finally had the chance. A man has to live some time."

This man feels the need of contrasts so strongly that he believes such a need to be innate in human nature. In his own view, human beings always want changes:

"I think we just want things to keep changing. Not many people would want everything to be the same... Many of the people who live here rearrange their furniture, exchanging some pieces, three times a year or more. It mustn't be the same old stuff always, or they'd get fed up with it. I've watched the women in this appartment block, pulling at chairs and tables and carpets, and when their husbands came home everything was topsy-turvy. I suppose it changes the atmosphere for a bit, and they're contented for a while..." (Single man, caretaker, aged 70.)

Depending on whether you wish to express contrasts or a "group taste," consequences will, of course, differ: contrasting patterns of consumption help define situations, special occasions, fashions, and the changing phases of life. The working-class man from a home where money was always tight loves clothes — in abundance — today. *The past* — "everything was darned and patched" — is contrasted with *the present* — "now I want the newest thing."

According to a young working-class man, you have a rough idea of the sort of thing you want, "the general sort of style." However, he emphasizes that once you've got the new things — wallpaper and wall-to-wall carpets, for instance — belonging to the style you had in mind, you're bound to want the latest thing. "You have to change to bring yourself up to date."

"Pinewood is the in thing now," said another young man from the working class. "The old-fashioned look is the newest style" or "vinyl wallpapers are what everyone's getting these days." Young working-class home-owners subscribed to a magazine in order to know the latest fashions; "I get to see the newest things automatically by subscribing to *Home and Leisure*".

A young working-class woman, making plans for her own house:

"Oak staves, that's the sort of wooden floor I want. Oh, I'm so sick of those squares I've got now, I've never liked them. *Now* I'm going to have oak staves."

Being aware of "the latest thing" helps a person feel that he or she is "still with it," living in the present — and marking contrasts with the aid of consumption.

Some Further Indices

In one of the interviews, a working-class woman (catering assistant, 35 years of age) stressed that she found it hard to see what would "go with" something else. "Neither my daughter nor I have any taste, you see..." A statement geared to defining attitudes which interviewees were confronted with ran, "Where clothes are concerned, I find it difficult to see what will 'go together' and what will not."

The proportion of interviewees who disagreed with the statement,, "Where clothes are concerned, I find it difficult to see what will 'go together' and what will not" (Percentage).

Single women in cities, middle class (40-47 years),	80
Young girls, upper middle class (16-18 years),	73
Young girls, working class (16-18 years),	47
Young housewives, in towns, working class (18-30 years),	46

Conversely, self-assurance in matters of dress, and "dress sense," were self-evident to most of the single middle-class women living in cities. Among them, a woman who admitted to not having any taste would seem odd. In the working class, though, this was nothing to be ashamed of.

Certain rules of taste are accepted in the middle-class groups. Not to be familiar with them would probably be felt to constitute a serious deficiency. Among working-class girls, however, the accusation of not having marked an occasion in a suitable manner amounts to an insult.

"And if anyone appears on the dance floor dressed in the most awful rags, one will look at her, I suppose, without saying anything mean. Or one might perhaps say to a friend, "Just look at her!" (Auxiliary nurse, aged 18)

Expressing group taste cannot be done mechanically, by wearing identical garments. Instead, it is a matter of a subtle "sensing" of the group style; copying does not come into it. However, those to whom contrasts between situations were essential felt free to copy and imitate.

The interviewees were asked to reply to the following question: "Have you seen many other people wearing exactly the same garment as one you've bought for yourself?"

The proportion of interviewees who replied in the affirmative to the question of whether they had seen many other people wearing exactly the same garment as one they had bought (Percentage).

Young girls, working class (16-18 years),	80
Young girls, middle class (16-18 years),	34

The discrepancy is clearly considerable.

This does not amount to saying that working-class girls found it particularly desirable to wear "things you see hanging on almost everybody." From time to time, though, it will happen. "Well, if you get your clothes at Hennes, you must expect everyone else to wear the same." (Auxiliary nurse, aged 18)

A working-class woman (catering assistant, aged 35) says,

"When I used to buy clothes, I'd go to EPA /the approximate Swedish equivalent of Woolworth's/. That was before I got married. And then, when I went to a dance, I'd see that almost every other girl would be wearing the dress I'd bought."

She added that while she did not wish to dress exactly like everyone else, it would happen, and not infrequently either.

"You've got to face it, you know... Hennes and that... Nearly half the girls you see wear the same thing. It's natural for people to buy similar stuff, after all."

It is important to observe that these different rationales of consumption by no means apply to clothes only. They could be discerned in different areas of consumption. Working-class groups would "tire of" their furniture and interior decorations more quickly than others.

A working-class man makes the following observations about himself,

"My goodness, I've been changing my furniture a lot. The different sets I've had! Green stuff, and red, and there was a time when everyone was supposed to have brown things... But when you've had a set for some time, you sort of tire of it... Then it's natural to pick another colour."

Against the background of this desire to counteract the feeling that "things are getting too ordinary" and that one is "in a rut" — the present being emphasized in contrast to the past — a further hypothesis may be set up: We may assume that a large proportion of the working-class group would agree with the statement, "A home is never really finished — one's bound to want something new all the time." The need for variation grows along with the urgency of the wish to satisfy "the contrast function".

This actually turned out to be the case: 84 and 79 per cent respectively in the two adult working-class groups agreed *entirely* with the statement that a home is never finished. Among middle-class women, however, the corresponding number was 66 per cent. It is true that the difference is not strikingly great (as was pointed out above, there is a need for change even when the group function is the essential factor). Still, the observable discrepancy does agree with the expected pattern. There are hence not many people who feel that innovations at home are something they are happy to ignore. "For a year maybe, but than you've got to be at it again," says a young working-class home-owner.

Not the End

The working class and the middle class have different ideas and patterns of consumption—the first in accordance with *the group rationale* and the second in accordance with *the contrast rationale*. The dissimilar modes of expression, or "languages," seem to adhere to a distinction which Simmel once drew up in respect of fashion about how the mode of expression in consumption unifies circles and creates dividing lines between situations. But, where do we go from there?

As I pointed out in the beginning of this chapter, though, patterns of consumption are a matter of "to be and not to be." No individual belongs *wholly* to a certain social category — and the outside part is never separated from the inside part.

It seems to me that the two rationales should be contemplated together and that their interrelationship actually embodies a kind of contradiction. In fact, both languages are present in both groups; and — viewed from a Simmelean perspective — either language serves to clarify the mode of expression contained in the other.

Of course, the two dissimilar functions are not opposites *per se*. As a result of their highly concrete social distribution, however, these two rationales — the group function and the contrast function — actually become contradictory. After all, the fact that they represent the very dissimilar social implications inherent in the expression of consumption on the part of two classes is not insignificant. The dual rationales for consumption has a parallel existence in both groups.

A middle-class girl discerns the norms of her social circle. But she also knows that the norms of the group are forever changing and that every social occasion provides different group norms. In that sense she must also know the consumption language of contrasts.

On the other hand, in the working-class groups consumption must, of course, also cater to group tastes. After all, what constitutes proper social contrasting is — inevitably — defined within the framework of the "own" group. Hence, the same line of reasoning must be adopted here: norms do exist in the working classes; but they do not make up the meaning of the "own" language. However, they reinforce their opposite. That makes it especially vital for consumption to give clear expression to contrasts between times and occasions.

Note

1. The material consists of 50 taped interviews and 314 structured ones concerning consumer attitudes, behaviour, and values. Six survey groups assumed to be strategic in terms of a study of consumption problems were selected. These different groups were defined beforehand, for example the two groups of young girls (16-18 years), one upper-middle-class and the other working-class, consisting of about 50 girls in each group. Fifty of these were interviewed. The survey was conducted in May 1975. The investigation was sponsored by the Swedish Governmental Department for Consumer Affairs.

II

The Oppositions within a Phenomenon Become a Motor, Inducing Change

6

The Motor Forces in Modern Fashion

*If the effect that one element produces upon another
then becomes a cause that reflects back as an effect
upon the former, which in turn repeats the process
by becoming a cause of retroaction, then we have a
model of genuine infinity in activity. Here is an
immanent infinity comparable to that of the circle...* [1]
Georg Simmel on The Philosophy of Money

In 1969, Herbert Blumer encouraged sociologists to undertake research on fashion: "This paper is an invitation to sociologists to take seriously the topic of fashion." Up to then, few sociologists except Simmel (1957), Sapir (1931) and Lang & Lang (1961) had, according to Blumer, taken more than a casual interest in the topic.

This lack of sociological analysis verges on the peculiar, especially as fashion is empirically intrusive today. In everyday life, we experience the changes of fashion in every possible context — changes in appearance, dress, interior decoration, food, Christian names, therapies for alcoholics, scientific perspectives, and popular expressions.

Fashion is by definition perpetual change, what Quentin Bell calls "the grand motor force of taste" (Bell 1976, p. 89). But what creates the energy that impels this motor? Are there even inherent traits, special qualities characteristic of the social phenomenon of fashion *per se*, which may bring about changes?

Starting from a number of empirical studies on fashions — food fashions, furniture fashions, Christian-name fashions (Sellerberg 1979,

1982, 1984, 1987) — I will contrast "modern" fashion with "classic" fashion. My main question is: What are the particular "motor" forces propelling the changes in modern fashion?

The Problem: The Dynamics of Modern Fashion

Simmel used the metaphor of the circle or curve to describe one of the ways in which the processes of social interaction unfold. Some Simmel scholars have also made specific attempts to discern various circular processes of social interaction (Nedelmann 1984, p.7). Nedelmann writes:

> If we accept that the processes of social interaction can unfold in a way which is analogous to the formation of a circle, this would imply that these processes create their own momentum; they are, to use a term which is difficult to translate, *eigendynamisch*. (Nedelmann 1987, p. 3)

Nedelmann's aim is a general one. She wishes to demonstrate the dynamic properties inherent in social interaction generally. Nedelmann particularly focuses on the type of forces which Simmel himself described with reference to the metaphor of the circle. (Simmel 1978, p. 119) This *Eigendynamik* is characteristic of the continual changes of fashion. She shows that

> . . . Simmel's perceptive and succinct analysis of the world of fashion is not merely an exotic contribution to the sociology of aestethics, but also contributes to the general theory of social action, or, to put it more precisely, to the theory of *Eigendynamik* or autonomous processes of social interaction. (Nedelmann 1987, p. 2)

My analysis of modern fashion will be an example of autonomous dynamics of this particular kind. Fashion produces emergent properties that reinforce and stabilize an ongoing process of circular stimulation. Thus, through its own very characteristics, fashion seems to become its own motor force.

Classic Versus Modern Fashion

In this discussion, fashion today will be contrasted with fashion as it used to be. Earlier and modern fashions are, quite simply, different social phenomena. Realizing this, Blumer emphasizes that difference by means of the subtitle of his article "Fashion: From Class Differentiation to Collective Selection" (Blumer 1969).

Thus, the way in which the classics — e.g. Veblen, Simmel, Sapir — regarded the fashion of their time consisted in interpreting it from a class-differentiation perspective. Veblen is perhaps the most explicit: To Veblen, but also to Simmel, the energy of fashion lay in its being the expressions of social distance by the upper classes towards other classes; a social elite emphasizes its particular social position by continuous changes in outward appearance. The perpetual shifts are due to the fact that after a certain time, these expressions of the elite spread to other groups, thus losing their original social connection. The fashion cycle will be repeated anew, now with something else to signify the social distance. These analyses stressed the class basis of fashion. Other interpreters who have analyzed fashion from a similar perspective are Nystroem (1928), Bell (1976), Fallers (1954), Barber and Lobel (1952).

These interpretations cannot, however, be applied to fashion as it is at present. One presupposition of the class-differentiation perspective is, for example, that most members of the various social classes in society want the signs of the social elite for themselves, in that sense possessing a uniform taste. However, this is a much too one-dimensional perspective (Alberoni 1946; Burns 1966, p. 323). Consequently, empirical studies on present-day fashions have shown that such unity is not characteristic of the consumer tastes of various social groups today (Sellerberg 1976, 1978, 1979, 1982). Today's fashion cannot be interpreted as status differentiations and trickle-down processes. (Munthers 1977) These classic forces in changing fashions seem not to agree with the empirical findings of our time (Horowitz 1975, King 1973).

Classical Dualism

Simmel's interpretations of the fashion of his time identify a primary pair, that of conformity and differentiation. Secondly, fashion struggles both upwards towards the surface, where it is shallow, and down to the deepest concerns of human beings. Paradoxically, in fashion the personal could, according to Simmel, be expressed by means of extreme imitation. Another pair of opposite forces is that fashion is both destructive and constructive. According to yet another set of opposites, we are superordinate to the laws of fashion in that we can use them for our own aims and for the social expressions we need at the moment. On the other hand, we are very clearly subordinate to fashion; sometimes it seems as if fashion wants to demonstrate its superordination by prescribing the particularly strange and impractical, and we obediently accept even the most obstruse styles, etc.

These opposite forces constitute dualistic tendencies: they counteract each other and actually stimulate each other in doing so, creating a kind of circular stimulation and *Eigendynamik*.

The Dualism of Modern Fashion

On the one hand, the results of my empirical studies — as well as those of other surveys — oppose Simmel's class-differentiation perspective on fashion. Nor do other characteristic opposing tendencies in the kind of fashion he analyzed appear to be the most important ones in modern fashion.

On the other hand, though, my interpretations very clearly emanate from Simmel; on the basis of various current contexts, I have tried to ascertain central dualistic traits of modern fashion empirically, investigating the way in which they work as circular stimulations (Sellerberg 1979, 1982, 1984, 1987):

- Fashion reduces social complexity. At the same time, due to its way of functioning, it generates complexity, e.g. more subtle distinctions. — And, once again, this creates a need for a reduction of this complexity.
- Fashion contains very precise rules and regulations regarding what is "in." In its functioning, however, fashion is subversive to every convention and authorized rule. — It thus also becomes subversive to its own established rules.
- On the one hand, fashion is indifferent to the material and practical. On the other hand, fashion feeds on and lives through the very concrete.
- Our attitude towards fashion today consists both of intense involvement and detachment; taken together, this pair forms an attitude of restrained involvement, a commitment which is constantly held back.
- Fashion involves responsibility as well as freedom from responsibility.
- Fashion is both accessible and inaccessible.

• Fashion gives authenticity to the present. It also gives the fashion of the past an air of unreality and inauthenticity.

Fashion reduces social complexity. At the same time, as a result of its way of functioning, it generates complexity and increased differentiation.
One main force on the part of modern fashion seems to be a tendency to reduce multiplicity and an indecisiveness in respect of alternatives in various extant social contexts.

The breeding-ground of modern fashion is a situation just like the one we have today: traditional rules have lost some of their *raison d'être*. In situations where there are no timeless rules to be obeyed, fashion draws its own contours describing what is "right," what has "that certain something," what is necessary, healthy, etc. Fashion temporarily orders the undecided.

The complexity and multiplicity that exist in most areas in society will necessarily give rise to various social instruments geared to reducing complexity (Luhmann 1979). One of these instruments is fashion. Paradoxically, however, this temporary reduction of complexity and creation of order often occurs by way of an even greater differentiation, and as a result of more precise distinctions being established. Thus, Roland Barthes has indicated how fashion journalists involved in this process are continually developing a new and ever more differentiating language. One important function of this language, and of these new distinctions, is to consign the previous fashion to oblivion (Barthes 1985; König 1974).

The big furniture company IKEA has an employee who is responsible for naming the new products. This has become a difficult task. "We have such a large assortment. The supply of names seems to have come to an end." (Möbler & Miljö, (Furniture & Environment), 1977, No.3:7) Besides, fashion may specify what is new by prescribing a certain combination of the "old" with just the "right" novelty. Alternatively, the new fashion may be defined by means of prescribing a very particular subcategory of what was formerly in fashion. The differentiation and greater complexity of fashion is thus created through various means.

On the one hand, fashion reduces complexity by spotlighting something as being the most interesting, the most practical, or simply that which is "in." On the other hand, in this very process fashion creates new boundaries and new differentiations with the help of language, concepts or new words.

An example which was felt to be of great interest in the mid-70's : the linguistic development of types of flour, "new" varieties of grain and new methods of treatment. In an advertisement from one of the larger mills, the following new types were presented at a certain point in time: 1) Rye. Whole grains, made by pressing steam-prepared rye lightly between rollers. 2) Crushed Wheat. A wholemeal product which gives the bread a coarser quality. 3) Crushed Rye. The taste is richer than that of crushed wheat. 4) Cut Wheat. Cut in pieces for quicker liquid absorption. 5) Cut Rye. Gives a coarser quality to the bread and a richer taste than with cut wheat. 6) "Sport-Flour" Wheat. All parts of the hull are included in order to make the product more rich in fibers. 7) "Sport-Flour" Rye. The bread has a richer taste than that of wheat bread. — These were only a few of many varieties mentioned. The above illustration from flour advertising was taken from my study of food fashions.

At that time, there was great interest in varieties of whole-grain flour (Sellerberg 1982; see also Rykwert 1977, p. 57). However, with the passing of time, these particular varities were dismissed as passé, uninteresting, "out," strange, or whatever.

In another study my subject was fashions in interior decoration (Sellerberg 1979). The study reflects the changes presented in interior-decoration catalogues and journals, year by year. Where wooden furniture is concerned, particularly good potentialities would seem to exist with regard to specifications and developments, that is, differentiations. A type of wood which used to be à la mode may be specified, and one of its varieties, with a certain precisely defined nuance in the finish, etc., comes into fashion. In this area, specifications also often seem to concern a certain country of origin or a particular period (or both), for example "English Colonial." In the differentiation process, the necessary boundaries around what is now "in" are drawn. And they are drawn with special severity against what was "in" yesterday.

In these two opposing tendencies, a kind of motor of change is located: fashion reduces and generates its own complexity, change being inherent in the very nature of fashion.

Fashion consists of very precise rules and prescriptions regarding what it authorizes as being "in." In its functioning, however, fashion is subversive to authorities.

An acquaintance of mine, a Polish immigrant, was angry. His son and daughter-in-law delayed their decision on a name for their newborn baby. He couldn't understand why the young couple had to discuss it with friends and consult books to find the right name. "My parents were illiterate, it's true. But they needed no books. They could still give fine names to their children."

Why, then, did our ancestors have no such problems? Because for a long time — up to rather recently — it was taken for granted that a newborn baby should be named after older relatives. Traditional rules for name-giving were widely spread in Western Europe: the oldest son should be named after his father's father, the next son should be named after his mother's father, the other children should get their names from other relatives. This tradition — the rule for hundreds of years — has been a handy instrument for historians and genealogists when charting sometimes complicated relationships. Some of these rules used to be particularly inviolable. If a father died before his son was born, the son should unconditionally be named after him. If a widow remarried, her first newborn son should be named after her late first husband. Towards the end of the eighteenth century, however, this long-lasting tradition was gradually modified. Now the number of names in use increased rapidly. Of course, parents did not entirely stop naming their babies after older relatives. The important thing in this context is that the rules were no longer taken for granted. This fact entailed a very decisive change. Now names had to be very deliberately chosen by the parents. (I have made a study of fashions in Christian names in Sweden, reported in Sellerberg, 1987.) The overall conclusion to be drawn from this is that when authoritative rules — of whatever kind — no longer seem valid, there is room for the operations of fashion (Blumer 1969). Now fashion — in firmly authoritative rules — defines what is "in" and appropriate: "A café is the thing this year." Current fashion is presented in categorical imperatives. The arrival of spring is accompanied by such slogans as: "The female body should be seen," "Now: Orange to Suntanned Skin," "This year: Broad-shouldered Gentlemen."

These are short-lived imperatives, though. The reason for their impermanence is that fashion, generally speaking, is characteristically inconsistent with and subversive to every authoritative and long-lasting rule of taste.

On the one hand, fashion is indifferent to the material and practical. On the other hand, the expressions of fashion are precise, apparent, sturdy and highly material.

Simmel emphasized the total indifference of fashion to usefulness and practicality — as well as to lack of utility and impracticality

(Simmel 1973). Fashion is unconcerned with either, and this is a condition for its existence, Sapir says (1931, pp. 139-144). Every fashion is hence, fundamentally speaking, something that cannot be put to use for any definite purpose and in that sense unnecessary. The coming fashion is, materially and practically, as "use-less" as the old.

On the other hand, new practicalities are often emphasized in fashion advertisements. In my food-fashion project, I discerned the characteristics of advertising for stoves: "The stove of the year," or some other piece of kitchen equipment of "this winter," was presented with new stop-watches, automatic boiling-plates and other gadgets and qualities. Socially, however, these practicalities do not primarily mark function but newness. At a certain point in time, the finer points of the "new" stove represent the latest thing. These new functions served to set the stove of the year apart from last year's models. Yesterday's fashions are a cemetery for defunct practicalities. But irrespective of whatever practicality — or impracticality — they may possess, fashions are bound to lose this particular social significance — that is, their modernity. The process is inevitable: The utility functions marked the essential difference from last year's product, and their possible practicality becomes utterly irrelevant (as, in fact, it was all along).

On the other hand, fashion utilizes the practical. It expresses its modernity through — and by means of — the material. What is new is thus made materialized, conspicuous and visually evident. — As I mentioned above, I studied fashions in bread flour and the related advertisements. When very coarse bread became à la mode, coarseness became visually important too. In the descriptions of different flours it is indicated, with great visual clarity, how certain products should be used. There were particular mixtures in which the bread should be rolled, thereby helping to emphasize the particular inside coarseness of the bread in question. At this time the fashion of coarseness in food developed its own esthetics: Grains and fibers were also made into visual decorations. Restaurants at this time advertised their new authentic products such as wholemeal bread, bran cakes and coarsely chopped salad in wooden bowls (Rykwert 1977, p. 57). The precise language of fashion makes us distinguish in constantly changing ways. Brown describes language as a mold shaping the mind, as well as a code connecting minds (Brown 1967, p. 314).

On the one hand, then, fashions consist of these highly material distinctions. On the other hand, they develop freely on this material ground. Actually, material development and differentiations are not the real issue after all. Fashion must have this particular freedom, too. Its unpredictability is therefore guaranteed; you cannot conclude that something will last merely because it is practical and functions well. Where fashions are concerned, it must not ever be possible to draw tenable conclusions.

Today, our attitude in respect of fashion consists of intensity and involvement as well as of distance and detachment.

At a certain point in time, a particular fashion engages and interests us. But our relationship to what is in fashion also includes distance; both distance and attraction are characteristic of attitudes to fashion.

The necessary distance to what is fashionable is created in a variety of ways: It may be guaranteed by the fact that the fashionable object or style was taken from somewhere distant — a bygone historical period, a faraway country, or a social context far removed from our own. In order to establish a distance, fashion may decree that the "old" fashion be redesigned. This may be achieved by means of a new way of combining familiar, everyday phenomena. It is also possible for the element of distance to operate in such a way that we pick a certain kind of fashion in a deliberately non-serious, ironic frame of mind. Interest and distance, distance and attraction make up our attitude to what is fashionable. Hence, our way of relating to current fashions incorporates different strategies to keep the necessary distance in spite of our interest. Conversely, for that matter, it might embody strategies geared to maintaining interest in spite of distance.

In a previous investigation I described food fashions by analyzing the content of magazines on food and cookery books: Food à la mode is certainly taken from very different corners of the earth, from various historical periods and from remote social conditions (Sellerberg 1982).

These temporary appearances of phenomena originally belonging to distant cultures and times were also very noticeable in my study of interior-decorating fashions: Swedish wallpaper producers planned their coming campaigns with the help of the National Department of Antiquities (Sellerberg 1979). Consequently, our preference for what is distant — in various ways — involves the very special attitude which Simmel described as an esthetic relation; modern man relates to surrounding objects by transforming them into a kind of art object:

All these forms, familiar to all the arts, place us at a distance from the substance of things; they speak to us "as from afar"; reality is touched not with direct confidence but with fingertips that are immediately withdrawn (Simmel 1978, p. 474).

The importance of distance to what is in fashion means that the exotic, the particularly unusual, etc., may well become the latest thing. Objects and styles that are ugly, particularly bad, silly and awkward come into fashion. One example is the so-called cult movies, or other "cult objects."

Accordingly, we appropriate fashions with interest but at the same time without internalizing, a manner of reacting which Simmel once called "a child of thought and thoughtlessness" (Simmel 1973, p. 173). Often we do the fashionable thing; but sometimes, as is frequently the case with cult objects, it is enough to know about it. We may thus be *au courant* by very consciously choosing the fashionable, but only doing so outwardly, or by speaking of a fashionable phenomenon and displaying our familiarity with it.

Here I have emphasized the importance of distance in attitudes to fashion. This has seemed particularly vital to me, as fashion has frequently been regarded as the opposite: an expression of interest, as in crazes and mass psychosis in taste. In my empirical studies, a particular mode of speaking of fashion became evident: "Now we are living in a certain period," this or that has "caught on," "boomed," or turned out to be "quite fun." The choice of words suggests impermanence and an element of chance. The vocabulary indicates a kind of self-consciousness, too.

Thus it has been wrongly supposed that fashion is followed unpremeditatedly. Fashion behavior has been looked upon as a craze: people do what everybody else does, without thinking about it. On the contrary, however, fashion behavior is premeditated to a considerable extent. It appears to me to be a sign of the times that so many theories on the self-consciousness of modern man — e.g. on narcissism and self-reflexivity — have been published during the last few decades (Lasch 1978; Lifton 1971; Ziehe 1984 are typical representatives). When it comes to fashion, those sociologists who talk about our "taken-for-granted attitude" in everyday life hence seem to be wrong. (For example, Berger & Luckmann 1967.)

In respect of fashion, we consciously decide "now this is what counts." Conversely, our attitude to tradition was completely different; you cannot choose that which is taken for granted. Now we are establishing a distance to many things that used to be thoroughly familiar, self-evident and never questioned. "For instance, we make decisions on how further (subordinate) decisions are to be made; we engage in learning how to learn and in teaching how to teach" (Poggi 1979, p. xiii). — This might even apply to choices concerning the best way of making choices. Poggi has pointed to this modern reflexive attitude: "Modernity also intensifies the recourse to *'reflexity'as a strategy for complexity reduction*, that intensifies the application of given reductive devices to themselves" (Poggi, ibid).

Fashion means a transitory interest. Where fashion is concerned, we consequently view our own engagement from a distance. This supplies a background to the element of self-consciousness in our attitude to fashion. At the very time when we are at the peak of interest, we know that the whole thing is transient.

As a result of the significance of both dimensions — distance and interest — , one strategy consists in being moderately interested in fashion. This also means that two attitudes in fashion seem most unbecoming and wrong: the first is to be too interested; the other is to be uninterested. Those who are too fashion-conscious easily become the object of ridicule: the necessary distance to what is in fashion has been lost. As Pascal once wrote: "The wise man is never first to follow, nor the last to keep" (Pascal cited by Midgley, 1973:415).

In our relationship to fashion we are, on the one hand, engaged as participants at a certain time, during an epoch, and in the present. On the other hand, we must be ready for change — and for tomorrow's engagements.

Fashion involves responsibility as well as freedom from responsibility.
In my empirical studies (Sellerberg 1979, 1982), an expression commonly used by interviewees was that you ought to be with it, "you ought to know about the latest thing." These expressions could sound like sighs; it was a responsibility to keep up with the current fashion — in which area depended, of course, upon the individual. In a newspaper interview, a researcher in the liberal arts states the duty of being in the picture, thereby indicating the importance of the Basle exhibition to him: "To anybody who believes it is important to know what is 'in' in art and who wants to keep up with trends, the information conveyed by the Basle exhibition can be useful."

In these contexts, the serious and prudent component inherent in the ambition to be "in fashion" becomes particularly evident. It is respectable to be fashionable; it is even our responsibility to be "with it."

On the other hand, fashion behavior is also associated with a particular freedom from responsibility. In the survey on interior decoration, I contrasted an attitude to fashion with rules on good taste in a context of exclusivity. Interviews illustrated how fashion gave relief from responsibility. The norms of exclusivity, though, involved no such freedom for interior decorators. In interviews with them, interior decorators were accused of not putting their talents to profitable use, not making the best of their apartments, not creating atmosphere, not expressing personality and so on.

By contrast to these exclusivity rules, the rules of fashion were clear and accessible. Adhering to them was a less complicated business and — an important point — whoever went along with what was fashionable was "discharged from liability" as a result. The interviews illustrated Simmel's statement that fashion frees from responsibility (Simmel 1957). Fashion can thus prescribe that we behave indecorously, e.g. even show our underwear. "The latest thing in underwear: wear something underneath and show others what it is." To those who follow the rules of fashion, the responsibility is no longer theirs.

In the context of fashion we are allowed to flirt with the unconventional and the socially dangerous. It is only a flirt, though; where fashion is concerned, the social peril seems to disappear. Wilson provides the example of the boundary between men's and women's clothes. Fashion has blurred the boundaries, so that from one point of view, in our way of dressing fashionably, we are flirting with transvestitism. At the same time, however, the phenomenon loses its original dangerousness when it occurs in connexion with fashion. Being fashionable, it is no longer the responsibility of the individual (Wilson 1985).

Fashion Is Both Accessible and Inaccessible

On the one hand, fashion is open and accessible; on the other, it is hidden, inaccessible and always surprising.

Fashion rules are openly presented. In the study of interior decoration I contrasted this openness of fashion with the difficulty of access that characterizes the rules of exclusivity. In that study, which investigated the preferences of interior decorators from different social classes, a group from the upper class was very anxious to emphasize that they never furnished according to fashion (Sellerberg 1979). Instead they referred to good taste, to what I call exclusivity rules. Their opinions about what constitutes good interior decoration were varied, including ideas such as "you should aim towards unity and wholeness." Or "was the right atmosphere created? Was personality expressed? Were the right pieces of furniture combined? Were the items well-balanced?" In short, the exclusivity rules were difficult to interpret and seemed inaccessible to an outsider. These norms did not embody any directions as to how they should be applied. They seemed unattainable and closed against the outside, and thereby exclusivity was secured.

The contrary applies to fashion. Its distinctions are very openly, even intrusively presented. Novelties and contrasts are emphasized and visualized. Being in fashion often means going to extremes. Articles on fashion in the weeklies tell you: "Fashion is made up of contrasts. It's a matter of pushing the limits. For without boldness and visual impact, there will be no fashion." It is stated that contrast is the password, and contrasts make differences evident. Those who are interested can look in papers, magazines and catalogues or take part in conferences, shows, seminars, exhibitions. The fashion supplement states in exact terms:

> "The Gandhi outfit," a lightweight, wide, long, rustling coat, is back in flamboyant colors. Combine it with a mini skirt and it's the very height of fashion. Or wear a short, snug sweater with one of the extremely popular wide shirts this spring. Put an over-sized vest over this shirt, and new visual impressions and proportions are created.

The distinctions of fashion being open and exact, it follows that you can be fashionable without believing in — and actually also without doing — that which is in fashion. It may often be enough to *know* about the new phenomena, thus being able to discuss fashion. Fashion constitutes a social structure based on information — those who know and those who do not know what is "in" at a given moment. If you want to be "with it," it is easy to make use of this accessible heap of information.

However, unpredictability — and in this sense inaccessibility — is a chief characteristic of fashion, too. Fashion must, in the end, surprise — or at any rate contain the possibility of surprise. Many have tried — in different areas — to plan, predict and secure fashion. Still, fashion should express the present, that which is actually happening, and the present can never be represented and signified by what could be planned yesterday. In the end, then, despite being overly explicit, fashion must also be unattainable. Well-planned commercial fashion may make a hit, it's true; but so may the unplanned.

Attempts to determine the origins of a particular fashion are numerous, and they have certainly yielded important information. Fashion researchers have tried to chart the conditions and rules pertaining to the development of certain fashions (Brenninkmeyer 1973; Carman 1973; Danger 1973; Koplin & Schiffer 1948; Reynold 1968; Richardson & Kroeber 1940; Robinson 1958; Young 1937). The length of skirts, the shapes of beards as well as car designs have been placed along a temporal dimension in order to make a possible pattern visible. Sometimes it is possible to chart the history of a fashion, perceiving how fashions actually build upon each other.

Interpretations aimed at tracing the synchrony of fashion in its relation to an era and the spirit of the times have been attempted. (See for example the works by the Swedish philosopher Sven-Eric Liedman.) Fashion is viewed as a system of signs by Roland Barthes, for example, in his already classical *The fashion system* (1985). However, in these interpretations — the synchronic as well as the diachronic-historical ones — inexplicable elements remain. Blumer states that the collective selection process in fashion seems mysterious to us. He maintains, however, that it seems mysterious because we fail to understand it (Blumer 1969). I would like to add that we never will understand it in the sense of being able to chart it and secure its development.

Fashion gives authenticity to the present. It also gives past fashions an air of unreality and non-authenticity.

At a certain time, fashion makes the occasional and limited seem natural and general (Barthes 1960). The cut of a dress, the new "in" word, the dominating judgement of an art style appear evident and necessarily rational. The Swedish sociologist Johan Asplund has described changing trends in the publication of making-the-best-of-yourself books. He describes the courses, conferences and seminars which are "in" at a certain point in time. Asplund makes an important observation concerning this material: these up-to-date pieces of advice and ideas on the right way of living always claim to be general and timeless. These ever-changing rules for living were presented as if they were universal, too, and could be applied to anybody. Actually, they involved management and leadership and only concerned a limited group of people.

This, however, seems to be something of a universal feature in modern fashions. Their rules are of a general character: "This is the way we dress this spring." Even if it actually concerns only a few, fashion appears as omnipresent, "that is the 'in' thing now." The present fashion is experienced as natural and authentic. By contrast, that of yesterday seems funny, strange and, above all, unreal: "How could we?"

Fashion rules our conception of the authentic. A bygone fashion as it is represented in movies, for example, seems unauthentic unless it is also filtered through the present fashion. The particular historical style reproduced in a movie inevitably seems to include important traits of the current fashion. "The Birth of a Nation" made by D.W. Griffiths in 1915 and "Gone with the Wind," made in 1939, both endeavor to show us what Americans looked like at the time of the beginning of the Civil War in 1861. The film-makers had an abundance of evidence, photographs, pictures, actual specimens of costumes, and the recollections of old people who had lived through that period. Still, the two versions are completely dissimilar. Bell states, "Miriam Cooper wears deflated versions of the crinoline, broad-waisted, flat-chested and very close in their floppy, unironed, unfitted way to the Paris fashion for 1916. Vivien Leigh in her incredibly broad shoulders, her 'page-boy' hair style, is very much in the fashion of 1939" (Bell 1976, pp. 78-83).

When an actor is dressed in an historical costume, the people in charge try to make the things represented as beautiful as they can while, at the same time, making them as historically correct as possible. But these two aims are incompatible. The more we beautify according to our taste and the present fashion, the more we remove the reconstruction from the prevailing taste of the time we wanted to recreate (See Bell 1976, p. 87). Once they have passed their "boom" and lost their modernity, objects, concepts, social movements and other social phenomena seem inauthentic and "play-acted." Pieces of furniture and other domestic appliances which signified modernity when they were bought subsequently lose this meaning completely. Asplund drew up a list of fashionable phenomena — ideas, concepts and people — at different times. Those were the times of...

New Thinking, Personal Development, The Nearness of Life and Death, Small Is Beautiful, New View of Human Nature, To Grow and Develop, To Care, Literature Helps Me With My Sentiments and Opinions, R.D. Laing, Man is Fantastic, Love Yourself, Androgynous Man, Assertiveness, I Believe in Ivan Illich, Jane Fonda's Workout, Biofeedback, Autogenous Training, Reflexo-Therapy, Balancing of the Body, Macrobiotics, Manipulating Treatment, Megatrends, Intrapreneur, Time Planning, Live in This Moment. (Asplund 1984)

These concepts now stand for obsolete fashions and hence appear unreal and illusory.

Concluding Discussion about the Motor Forces of Fashion

First, fashion both reduces and generates social complexity. In this sense, it functions as a perpetuum mobile, producing its own fuel for change. Second, fashion is anti-authoritarian and entails continual breaks away from what is established. These breaks, however, assume their own, highly authoritarian form. "This is the thing right now." Third, our relationship to fashion consists of both distance and attraction; in our interest and involvement we are ready to change in order to loosen the grip of the current fashion. Fourth, our going along with fashion seems to be connected with particular responsibility: You *should* be aware of the latest thing. That attitude appears to be a condition for fashion's expansion to highly respected and serious areas. On the other hand, fashion means freedom from responsibility. In this loosening of the straight-jacket of dutifulness, fashion provides space for breaks against conventions and for daring experiments. Fifth, fashion is open and accessible in its representations while being secretive and inaccessible at the same time. (If it had not been beyond reach before its possible "hit," fashion could not have signified the newest thing and a break with yesterday.) Sixth, fashion makes the present appear authentic and real, imparting an element of unreality to the fashions of the past.

Par définition, fashion consists in perpetual changes. Today, those changes happen quickly. The area of fashion seems to be expanding. Therefore it is particularly important to distinguish those properties of fashion which give rise to these fast changes and this expansion.

The answer is that pairs of dualistic tendencies, presented together, function as motor forces in this respect. They make fashion expand. They imply inevitable change. They give people incentives to go against convention, thus making up the social identity of modern fashion.

Changes of fashion involve most areas in society. It is important to describe these changes; but it is also vital to find out how this ongoing process affects the attitudes of human beings to their surroundings: If fashion constitutes an essential process of change in a society, the present and participating in the present become important to its members. Gabriel Tarde distinguished two main types of societies:

> In periods when custom is in the ascendant, men are more infatuated about their country than about their time; for it is the past which is pre-eminently praised. In ages when fashion rules, men are prouder, on the contrary, of their time than of their country. (Tarde 1903, p. 247)

In times when fashion rules, then, living and participating in the present is particularly important to individuals. Being in the picture, knowing about the latest thing in some area or other, is our key to this participation.

Note

1.   Simmel, Georg. *Philosophy of Money*, 1978, p. 119.

7

The Vacation Experience

*While it falls outside the context of life, it falls, with
the same movement, as it were, back into that
context again. . . It is a foreign body in our existence
which is yet somehow connected with the center.*

Georg Simmel on Adventure

This chapter is concerned with a modern experiential option, namely that of the vacation experience, and with the question in what this experience actually consists. This issue seems to me to be a historical novelty; in pre-industrial society, work was part and parcel of everyday life and there was no sense in which leisure was a separate section of the day (see Burns 1973, p. 43). Later, legally guaranteed vacations and shorter working-hours were, to begin with, associated with a predetermined — often religious — *use* of that particular time.

Only much later were individuals allowed to determine the use of their "own" leisure time for themselves. This change constitutes a major revolution. After all, predetermined leisure and a vacation planned by others clearly impede the emergence of the brittle and volatile vacation experience.

This analysis starts out from empirical findings derived from a study, conducted in the mid-seventies, of the vacation phenomenon (Sellerberg 1976a and 1976b). The relevant study reflects great and well-known differences between the ways in which people belonging to various social groups spent their vacations. For example, camping was very much a feature of the lifestyle of young working-class girls.

Percentage who went camping (N=100).

Young working-class girls (16-18 years old),	45
Young upper-middle-class girls (16-18 years old),	2

Many Swedes spend their holidays abroad. Still, my study indicated social differences between those who went on package tours and those who travelled on their own.

Percentage going abroad on their own (not a package holiday) (N=100).

Young upper-middle-class girls (16-18 years old),	50
Young working-class girls (16-18 years old),	10

The immediate reaction of most readers to this difference will probably be an attempt to perceive a concrete reason for it. Might it not, for instance, be due to economic considerations? Natural as this assumption may seem, it turned out to be dubious.

A study of the economic situation of young people in Sweden, conducted at that time, showed very few differences in terms of actual spending between socio-economic groups. In fact, the difference between the amount of money available to boys and girls respectively was of greater importance (Persson & Dahlgren 1978, p. 21).

Even so, of course, differences between these groups were great when it came to what people actually did while on holiday: what constituted the perfect vacation for one group was unthinkable to another.

This dissimilarity was especially patent in the taped interviews made alongside the structured ones: the former revealed the intense negative feelings associated with the ways in which other groups spent their holidays. For instance, middle-class girls would claim to "hate the Canary Islands and places like that." These girls were also decidedly anti-camping. To members of the working class, wilderness camping outside established sites appeared strange and unthinkable. ("Not seeing any people! Never!") There seemed to be an apprehensiveness lest the wrong choice might make the holiday impossible and inhibit the vacation experience.

Neither Direct nor Inverse

A number of comprehensive investigations of vacations have tried to explain — as well as to describe — these very dissimilar choices. Why are the middle class and the working class attracted by such different kinds of vacations? Two perspectives would appear to be helpful when it comes to explaining these differences. On the one hand, there are the "over-spill hypotheses." The type of work an individual does is directly reflected in his/her choice of vacation. Routine jobs, working with or close to automated machines, lead to routine vacations. In other words, this line of thought suggests a resemblance between a person's gainful employment and the kind of holiday that appeals to him/her. On the other hand, there are the contrast hypotheses: the choice of vacation is, in important aspects, a contrast to one's work; we search for vacations which are the opposite of our daily working life. Daily moderation and routine duties lead to a vacation characterized by liberality. However, in a summarizing account of these two interpretations — commenting upon the studies of, among others, Dumazedier and Crozier — Tom Burns states that both Dumazedier's Annecy studies and Crozier's survey of office workers reach the same conclusion —there is *no evidence of either a direct or an inverse relationship between work and leisure* (Burns 1973, p. 41).[my italics]

Instead, the differences where holidays are concerned seem to me to involve highly dissimilar and very deliberate choices. People choose differently in their striving for the vacation experience. What, then, is a vacation experience? What kinds of experiences are people really looking for when resorting to such dissimilar forms of vacations as "touristing?" What features are feared as totally "impossible" if the "wrong" type of vacation is chosen? What might destroy a vacation experience?

Early this century, Simmel analyzed the "adventurous" experience as a synthesis of opposites. Adventure experience must feature both known and familiar things *and* the unknown; it must embody an active mastery of *as well as* passive surrender to circumstances. In this context, it is natural to assume that vacations, too, may be a kind of adventure, sociologically speaking, and that the vacation experience must be similarly related to/distinct from our everyday non-vacation life.

If that is indeed the case, we are in fact also dealing with the relation of an experience to the whole of our life. One of two experiences which are not particularly different in substance, as far as we are able to show, may nevertheless be perceived as an "adventure" and the other not. The one received the designation denied the other because of this difference *in relation* to our life as a whole (Simmel 1965, p. 243). [my italics]

If we accept that we are dealing with a phenomenon which has a bearing on the whole of a person's life, we must, first of all, realize that what is a vacation for one person is not so for another.

Second, it follows that the different vacation options chosen by human beings really and essentially embody hopes for this vacation experience. The whole of a person's life is the issue, not the concrete content of a holiday.

> The decisive point about this fact is that the adventure, in its specific nature and charm, is a form of experiencing. The content of the experience does not make the adventure. (Simmel 1971, p.197)

Third — and this is a vital point — the combination of the familiar and the unknown entails an inevitable impermanence and elusiveness. We have all heard someone sighing disappointedly that her vacation, which was so carefully planned and on which so many hopes and wishes focused, did not turn out to be a true vacation at all. The synthesis, the balance was lost.

Fourth, this starting-point means that no particular predetermined vacation content can actually *guarantee* the experience in advance. The experience we crave is such that it just cannot be safeguarded and produced by dint of diligent planning.

And yet this chapter discusses the ways in which we will still be planning, making great efforts to select the appropriate kind of holiday so as to — in my view — ensure that we really do gain that vacation experience which cannot in fact ever be guaranteed. Thus, for instance, we may plan an experience supposed to embody the unexpected, new, and unplanned.

The Insecure Balance

As previous sections suggested, the vacation experience stands in a specific relation to ordinary life. However, this relation is not simply and unambiguously a matter of contrast or "over-spill."

When choosing a vacation, we attempt to achieve this precarious social "both-and" composition. The sought-for experience must be outside the usual continuity of life. Often, people in search of the vacation experience first try "to get away" in the physical sense. The games-playing world of camping, like other "play worlds," has a specialized, set-apart playing field which clearly demarcates it from everyday life (See Burch 1965, p. 605). However, this outside experience must also have an "inside" anchorage, and it must not be too unfamiliar; a combination is desired. Thus, for instance, campers — though isolated from the commitments of their ordinary lives — pursue many of the routines of everyday life (Burch 1965, p. 605).

Tourists are often criticized for not taking in the new and unfamiliar milieus ("tourists merely want to *recognize*"). In museums, they are said to be interested in recognizable if unfamiliar objects, such as ancient household equipment — "fancy baking with one of those!"; "that's when they had to do their own slaughtering!" — strange things which are still clearly associated with well-known functions. In art museums such as the Louvre, tourists look for La Gioconda, so well-known through reproductions but still new as a first-hand experience.

When visiting new places, tourists tend to go to the well-known districts — in Paris the Montmartre and Montparnasse, in London Soho and Trafalgar Square. When abroad, tourists walk along the well-known "tourist streets," for example the overcrowded passage from the Rialto to San Marco in Venice, or the "tourist walks" in the old city of Rhodes. This confined area — familiar in its old-town character — ends very abruptly, though: Adjacent streets have no appeal. They seem too strange, too out-of-the-way, and are thus empty of tourists.

A typical development can be found in popular Swedish-built hotels in the Mediterranean, where guests may cook (often partly with Swedish ingredients, bought in the Swedish shop located in the area) their own meals in the kitchenette allocated to the room. The vacation experience is the execution of these routine tasks — carried out in the exotic Southern European climate and environment.

The local representatives of tour operators do their best to help create these combinations — or syntheses, to use Simmel's term — of the unfamiliar and the intimate: the hotels on Majorca, by beaches lapped by the Mediterranean, treat guests to musical evenings where the best-known Swedish songs are sung; and there are after-beach shows imitating currently popular television entertainment. During evening dances, the sounds of Swedish folk tunes float over empty swimming-pools, and the passenger boarding the bus for a trip to the Old Town is exposed to the rhythms of the Swedish Top Ten, relayed by the Majorcan driver's tape-recorder. Accompanied by the notes played by dance orchestras back home, he/she travels among water-mills and cypresses. In connection with such phenomena as these, it has been argued that what we really want as tourists is to be safe at home, and that we are constantly searching for security represented by Swedish meat-balls and Swedish coffee. Even so, the familiar things themselves are not the point, or at least not the whole point. The really crucial phenomenon is the *combination*, the synthesis of the best-known *and* the exotic experience. The strange and unfamiliar is every bit as important. If it were not, the vacation experience would keel over and become too familiar, thereby losing its essential duality.

There are, however, other special features in this dualism. One is made up of actively mastering the well-known while passively receiving the new and unfamiliar. Simmel wrote about the synthesis of adventure as a vulnerable intermediate position "between the categories of activity and passivity, between what we conquer and what is given to us" (Simmel 1971, p. 192).

This brings us to the subject of the social distribution of different and highly concrete vacation skills: There are camping skills, caravan-site skills, package-holiday skills, summer-cottage vacation skills and skills for traveling around Europe on a Young People's Inter-Rail Card. We master a small selection of vacations. This mastery forms one aspect of the vacation experience. Still, the reward inherent in practising and mastering is not sufficient. It is a matter of surrendering oneself to the unknown, too...

Hence, a kind of tension is also present in holiday planning: the "other thing" has to be planned, too; we want to include the unknown, that which we are to surrender to. The synthesis may end up as hazardous mountain-climbing holidays in well-known company; caravan vacations where you meet some of the old inhabitants of the site while mingling with new ones; or mastering the routines of everyday life in out-of-the-way places.

We might say that these double qualities in the vacation experience interact with and reinforce each other. The familiar makes the search for the outside experience more important; the active mastering of known situations creates the — additional — wish to let go and deliver oneself up to circumstance.

Achieving the Synthesis

Our various "holiday backgrounds" influence our choice of vacation.

Drawing on them, we try to work out different plans for the vacation experience. One initial strategy is to look for situations, places, and surroundings where we may expect to experience this very "balanced" composition. In reality, the result is that the person who plans and arranges his/her vacation tries to guarantee improvisations and to secure some adequately proportioned risks. The middle-class girls I interviewed traveled around Europe using inter-rail cards. They didn't know beforehand where they were going or where they would stay. "I'm not going anywhere special, traveling freely." They really wanted to secure an insecure vacation and adventurous risk-taking. Too much security would have ruined every opportunity for the vacation experience they had in mind. The same may be said about the camping working-class girls: the familiar, the things they mastered, could be combined with new acquaintances in new places.

Another strategy we are apt to resort to as holiday-makers consist in orienting our experiences in the appropriate direction once we are on the spot, i.e. the holiday site. For instance, we may bring in our own representations of "known" and "unknown" so as to achieve the desired composition. We have strategies for this. For example, in a strange environment, we try to render the unknown familiar: we talk of "our" waiter, "our" hotel, etc. Travel agencies also intervene and facilitate this "trivialization." Certain shops are made to be "ours," as well as a selection of named restaurants. In these ways, the unknown, too, becomes familiar.

The Paradox

Still, all our efforts in this line embody an inevitable opposition and paradox: When planning and arranging vacations, we try to guarantee and secure a both-and combination.

Travel agencies, package-tour operators and tourist bureaux of various kinds also try to facilitate these attempts of ours. Here, however, we encounter another instance of the eternal dialectic described by Simmel: We try to realize the vacation experience with the aid of institutions — and at the same time, these attempts are always ultimately impeded by those same institutions. The reason for that is that these institutions, once in existence, tend towards autonomization, towards becoming stable creations — the very institutions that were to facilitate our vacation experience.

It must be borne in mind that every vacation experience calls for novelty, too. That is, after all, part and parcel of the vacation experience, "I know *too much*."

Consequently, every genuine vacation experience which an individual person has entails an unavoidable tipping of the balance: "Now, this has become familiar — too familiar, really." In this way, holidays consume themselves and demand change.

8

Subordinated under a Principle: Interaction in Geriatric Hospitals

*The fact that here a real interaction, at least an
immediate interaction, is precluded, seems to
deprive this form of the element of freedom.[1]*
Georg Simmel on Subordination Under a Principle

To be subordinate to a principle, a fixed schedule, etc., is — according to Simmel — the hardest kind of subordination, being the most rigid.

Field research for the current study took place in two Swedish geriatric hospitals, medical facilities specializing in the care of the elderly. Taped interviews and observations made in the eight wards were conducted by a post-graduate student, who was also a registered nurse, and by the author.[2]

After finishing a regular report (Sellerberg 1983) on the ways in which the patients liked various dishes served, and on what the staff thought about the service system (canteens, trays, etc.), I started a secondary analysis. At this stage, I discussed the stringency and centralization of rules for hospital administration — and in this case with reference to hospital food (Sellerberg 1986; Sellerberg 1989).

One general element in the Swedish welfare system, exemplified in these publically administered hospitals, is a high degree of centralized regulation. This also goes for the hospital food, both with regard to nutritional content and timing. Central norms for hospital food state the exact vitamin and nutrient content which every meal has to contain, in this case the meals served to elderly long-term-care patients (Sellerberg 1986). The correct timing of hospital meals is specified in what one hospital administrative unit refers to as "The Bible" in an interview — that is, the book *Hospital Diets*.

In the two Swedish hospitals, both patients and staff are *subordinated to a principle* — the fixed mealtime system.

From this perspective, the firmness of the superordinate rule forming a point of departure, the secondary analysis of interviews and observations offered ample illustrations of a very particular interaction pattern: on the one hand, the patients expressed their perspective in the way they waited for their food, as well as in the way they controlled the adherence of the staff to the established order; on the other hand, members of the staff expressively demonstrated that the schedule was a working scheme.

Nothing can be changed in the ruling order. However, certain symbolic expressions made by the parties — in their subordinate positions — seem to acquire a particular significance. From that perspective, restrictions affecting the possibilities for negotiation are of special interest.

Interactions between staff and patients have often been interpreted as negotiations between parties in different power positions (See for example, Strauss 1978; Sugrue 1982, pp. 280-292; Levy 1982, pp. 293-311; Kleinman 1982, pp. 312-327; Hall & Spencer-Hall 1982, pp. 328-349). Roth (1984, p. 113) describes a struggle resulting from attempts made by both parties to uphold their negotiated positions. A particular interpretative framework may, however, be applicable in one cultural context but less so in another.

In a comparison between US hospitals and hospitals outside the United States, Roemer and Friedman conclude that this pattern of high structuring that only characterizes a minority of general hospitals in the US is the prevailing one in Europe (1978, p. 322):

> To epitomize the entire pattern of European hospitals, compared with American, one may say that, being obviously older, the European hospital is a more crystallized system. — Ownership is more often by the government, and financing comes from large social insurance or public funds. Planning of construction and operation is more centralized. ... The whole hospital system is subject to national and regional planning that attempts deliberately to integrate the hospital into an overall system of medical care. (1978, pp. 329-330)

The basis of the negotiation perspective is that actions taken by the parties concerned can influence and change the relevant order. One essential aspect of the present analysis is that in the situation described here, the schedule cannot be changed or negotiated. Life in the two geriatric hospitals was organized around a non-negotiable daily schedule: the arrival and the departure of the food cart were very rigidly fixed. Both staff and patients showed an ingrained respect for this daily time schedule. In this sense, *both* staff and patients were subordinated to this firm and unyielding rule. If their strong commitment to the time rule had not existed, the particular power struggle between staff and patients as it is described below would not have arisen.

If negotiations are not an option, what kind of interaction takes place instead? This investigation suggests that in this characteristically inflexible situation, each party is eager to establish its particular perspective in relation to the superordinate rule.[3] In various situations, the staff emphasize that the time schedule is a *working* scheme. The patients, on their part, maintain that it is a mealtime system, and that it is their right to have their meals on time. There is little room for negotiations. But there is a latitude for *expressions*.

In the following analysis, the superordinate principle is associated with *expressivity*. Such a view goes against the conceptions of some classical thinkers. Simmel refers to Aristotle, who is said to have praised rule by law as "tó méson", implying that there should be moderation in all things, as well as impartiality and freedom from passions. By the same token, Plato had already recognized government by impersonal law as the best means for counteracting selfishness (Simmel 1964, p. 252).

This chapter stresses the contrary idea: in a situation where both parties are subordinated, certain emotional expressions are their only means of interaction.

Zerubavel: The Time Schedule and Group Relations

A total institution, as defined by Goffman (1961) and others is characterized — among other things — by the fact that daily activities are tightly scheduled. Furthermore, the sequence of activities is imposed "from the top" (Goffman 1961, p. 6). Like other total institutions, the two geriatric hospitals are thus examples of very firm "clock-work environments". (See Zerubavel 1981a, pp. 14-16 for the concept.) Most of the recurring activities follow a very rigid schedule. Patients are taken out of bed at a particular time and according to a scheduled order.

Bathing patients, the distribution of medicine, mealtimes, rounds, ward meetings, visiting hours, gymnastics, swimming, therapy... all have their scheduled times.

The interviews dealt with what appeared to be an especially important cog in this clock-work environment — the schedule for meals. The food cart arrived in the ward at a set time. After the meal, the cart passed by the ward on the scheduled minute, at which time the dishes and trays were loaded onto it and removed.

In this case, Zerubavel's term "clock-work environment" does not seem to be stringent enough. It was not only that mealtimes were very precisely established; another significant factor was the *intensity* with which both staff and patients discussed mealtimes and the trifling arrangements connected with them. One vital point in this context is that the superordinate rule is a *time* schedule. Zerubavel (1981a) regards temporal schedules as being linked to *group reactions* and, in consequence, to spokesmanship. Adhering to a schedule can be a means of solidifying in-group sentiments. People seemed to feel that it was their duty to keep on their guard for the good of their group, making sure that other parties were also subordinated to the time principle. In that sense, the analysis below does not deal with a power interaction between individuals but with a struggle between groups.

This struggle between the relevant groups — both in subordinated positions — will be discussed in the following sections: "The Interaction," "Staff Initiative or the Right to Extra Coffee," and "The Patients' Control in Doubt."

Two Group Perspectives

The same objective schedule appeared in a very different light to the two groups. What was work for the staff was a mealtime schedule for the patients. The consequences of this difference may be contemplated from a "figure-ground" perspective. What constitutes the background? What stands out in relief as a pattern? (Koffka 1935, p. 177-210). Everyone wanted to call attention to his own particular perspective. In various ways, the staff maintained *their* perspective, expressing their view that the time schedule was a facet of their job. As Zerubavel emphasizes, time schedules lead to group sentiments. In their descriptions of their working duties, the staff would employ technical terminology, thus making it absolutely clear that the descriptions referred to *work*. They reported the number of patients they had to "manage" within a certain period of time. "Five eaters," "four to supervise during the meal," etc. had to be managed within the established temporal framework.

Patients reacted and interacted by emphasizing their side of the schedule. They sat waiting for meals in a spirit of challenge. The mealtime schedule was probably particularly important to these geriatric patients. According to Roth (1963, p. 105), hospital schedule acquires particular importance for those who are chronically ill. He sees these patients as being on a "chronic side-track"; life in such a cul-de-sac is not like an ordinary career for hospital patients because it leads nowhere. It is only marked by what Roth calls a "failure timetable." In this situation, the hospital's time schedule acquires very great significance, as it splits "the long blocks of time into smaller, more manageable units" (Roth 1963, p. 12).

The Interaction

The interaction consisted of one part putting forward his/her perspective — and the other party answering and reacting by expressing and stressing his/hers.

The staff's perspective: Staff often used numbers and technical words. To them, the schedule constituted a co-ordinated system of working duties. One nurse said,

> "If things get delayed here, then we finish late. And then the hospital caretaker has to wait. And then things will be late in getting to the kitchen. Lots of times *we* get the blame!"

On occasion, the schedule was disrupted. Reactions among the staff were strong, and much discussion ensued. For example, if the patients' used trays were not placed on the cart on time, unwashed dishes and uneaten food were left in the ward until the next meal. The staff experienced such leftovers as discreditable. An LPN (practical nurse) was even of the opinion that no matter how you may alter the schedule, work will always be performed under pressure:

> "It's still such a *rush*. There are limits to the number of trays you can have left on the ward. So there's always some pressure on you to get as many trays as possible on to the cart."

In the interviews, the staff expressed their annoyance with the schedule. At a staff meeting, they criticized the obligation to feed patients within this restricted temporal framework. Sometimes they had to hurry patients along, almost force-feeding them in order to keep to their work schedule. Even if they regretted having to push the patients, they stressed the importance of adhering to the schedule:

" It's really like stuffing sausages. No small talk, only 'open wide now,' 'open wide now'..."

They described how rushed they could be. As one LPN said:

"You went around with a constant burning sensation in your stomach. I thought, 'I have to hurry.' Everything was so programmed. If anything happened to disturb the routines, well..."

The nurses pointed out that they feared unexpected events which could destroy the day's program. A practical nurse said, "If someone, for example, were to pull out a catheter..." Emergencies — patients, that is — disturbed the usual rhythm:

"We just hope that nothing else will happen. Like last Monday night, when Arvid fell on the floor just when the food cart arrived."

The staff emphasize that some unexpected events can cause the early-morning gruel, usually served between 6 and 7 a.m., to be delayed until close to 8 a.m. If, for instance, the night staff "have a death," normal temporal and working divisions are disarranged.

"If they got a death in the morning, no one gets fed, really. That's how it has to be... and so, it can take until 8, twenty past eight."

The patients' perspective: The patients were usually very particular about their mealtime schedule being followed. Most of them wanted to be up and dressed for breakfast, and almost all of them required help from the staff in the process of getting up. The staff describe how angry and disappointed the patients could be if the nurses did not have time to get them all ready:

"Then they all pushed their buttons. -'Aren't I going to get up soon?' 'I want to be up before breakfast.' Otherwise they won't eat! I remember lots of times when they were furious. They don't eat breakfast, and they won't accept it if we tell them that we have two or three new staff members, that we just don't have enough time to get them all up. 'Sure,' they say, 'we can lie here. It's OK.' If you go out, they look at the time, and if you stop and listen behind the door, you hear them saying to one another, 'It stinks!' "

The patients' anger when the mealtime schedule was not kept had far-reaching effects; according to staff, "If you didn't have enough time, they got so angry that you couldn't talk to them all day."

Members of the staff commented on the way in which patients always waited for their meals. "Most of them come out in plenty of time," a nurse said. "The patients sit in a group down there and wonder what's going to be served," she continued. An LPN said:

"They sit down there and wait. And gather together. It's the highlight of the day for them. You can see it. 'Cause they sit there long before it comes. Usually for an hour or so."

If something deviated from the schedule, the patients immediately remarked on it. The patients almost seemed to be "programmed," as the staff put it. Even those patients who were somewhat arteriosclerotic could get very anxious if the time schedule was not followed to the letter. An LPN says, "The patients can't stand it if things don't happen in the right order. Even the ones who aren't lucid." If there was a meal which did not arrive at the proper time, or which was perhaps even skipped, the patients who were not mentally alert became worried:

"And even the ones who are rather fuzzy... if they don't get their gruel one day, it's 'Nurse, I didn't get any gruel!' They know that they should have it before they get washed and it's time to get up."

The patients had a variety of ways in which to express demands that the staff hurry up. Staff were supposed to help them and make it possible for them to manage:

"They are in such a hurry to get out of there [the dining room], many of the patients. They have other appointments. They have to go to therapy. They have to go to the bathroom. They have to rest. They want to be first in the wheelchair line. [The 'chair line' consisted of a queue made up of all the wheel-chairs lined up in the corridor when the food was distributed.]"

Patients emphasized their side of the schedule in competing with one another. Such competition forced the staff to hurry up. In some wards, almost all the patients would demand quick assistance in going to the bathroom immediately after every meal. Some LPNs comment on the state of things on their wards:

"Just after breakfast and dinner. Then just about every one of them has to go. And so they push their buttons."

Another says:

"I think it's contagious. If a new one comes, she sees this. Bathroom, bathroom, bathroom! So soon it's bathroom! for the new one, too."

Within the rigid framework of the time schedule, this interaction of social markings acquires significance. When all the women patients want to go to the bathroom, it becomes particularly important to the staff to show and express that now is the time to collect dirty china and trays. Correspondingly, when the staff are busy collecting trays, it becomes extra important for all the women patients to get to the bathroom...

There are, of course, other ways in which the staff can express the importance of their side of the scheme. One way of emphasizing its character of a working schedule is to be busily and visibly engaged in extensive mealtime preparations. Directly after lunch, staff were already in a hurry to prepare the trays for afternoon coffee, scheduled to take place some hours later. Staff also prepared for the coming distribution of medicines. They made high "towers" of ready-filled medicine cups. In one instance, patients' medicine was prepared for weeks to come.

In this case too, however, the patients seemed to have an adequate response reaction ready: they changed their minds. In connection with the medicine distribution, to be sure, this response was not always practicable. But it was effective concerning other preparations — e.g.

what cakes with coffee, what kind of sandwich they wanted, etc. These demands for changes appeared primarily at breakfast and the evening meal, and they concerned sandwich fillings and what the patients wanted to drink - coffee, tea or milk. An LPN says:

"It often happens that you go in with a tray. Then they say, 'I don't want coffee today. Get me something else.' "

Or, as another LPN says:

"Sometimes you really get hell for the food you carry in."

Staff Initiative or the Right to Extra Coffee

The staff thus express their occupational perspective by referring to patients as "five to feed,""six to help," by resorting to extensive work preparations, and so on. Another type of expression consists in demonstrating that they are in charge of food distribution. This particular interaction between staff and patients will be presented below: staff mark their food-distribution initiative, and patients try to curb this emphasis. The discussion below, concerning an extra "surprise coffee," presents an interaction between staff who try to keep the initiative by means of surprising and patients who attempt to make this initiative into a controllable routine.

The "surprise coffee" was served on the staff's own initiative, above and beyond the time schedule. On some wards, the staff occasionally served this unscheduled coffee at about 11 o'clock in the morning. The idea was that when the staff had time, they would surprise the patients with extra coffee. However, the concept "surprise" implies an inherent variation. The additional coffee break should *not* be part of the daily routine; and as with every surprise, the surpriser has the initiative. The surprise coffee was an embryonic routine: the staff tried to maintain their surprise initiative, and the patients attempted to transform it into a permanent routine.

Staff from wards that had started "extra coffee" warned those who had not about the dangers of beginning such a program. The initiative created certain risks. After a while it tended to slide from staff to patients. One nurse supplied the following description:

"... coffee should only be for those who are up and around. *Only* those out here should have it. But it has become very important. Now they all come rolling along in their wheelchairs."

The informal surprise offered by the staff elicited an immediate reaction, as the patients tried —in different ways — to make the occasion into a routine, thereby rendering it observable and controllable. Staff said that it took "at most three weeks ... after that it is impossible to remove it." A nurse complained, "This coffee break, which should only be a treat, is now something we have as a ritual."
She continued:

"At first, we often did have the time. But then it got hectic for a while. And then they got so angry, you wouldn't believe it. 'What?! No 11 o'clock coffee?' "

However, the interaction of expressions went on: staff tried to counteract their loss of control. Different strategies were applied to stay in command of the situation. Staff decided, for example, that only *certain* categories of patients, *chosen* by the staff, should be given surprise coffee. "We only invite those who are sitting out there." On another ward, staff did not serve coffee to those who needed help when they ate and drank, and they emphasized that *they* were the ones who made the choice.

"Many patients stay in the ward, in their rooms. You don't go in there and ask. Instead it's the ones who sit out there.
—It's only the ones who sit in the dayroom and some who are in their rooms. As for the bed-ridden patients. . . we only give coffee to those who can sit and those who can drink themselves. So that it is something *extra*."

In another ward, the staff had decided to give coffee only to patients who had directly asked for it.

"Those who *ask* for it get coffee. If they don't ask, they don't get any. So it's just as well to leave well alone. 'Cause you're the one who gets stuck with it later. We think they nag. And they think that we're difficult because we don't give them coffee when they think we should."

In these heated discussions, the staff claimed that this was a general goal on the patients' part: they always wanted to introduce new elements into the established schedule. One nurse said:

"Everything becomes routine here! Fast as hell. It just takes one or two weeks and then they're on to it."

This ward interaction, with one party striving to keep behavior informal (and therefore uncontrollable by the other party) and the other trying to make the informal formal and controllable, seemed to constitute a general pattern. For example, the staff served the patients food in a certain order. The patients tried to make this order into a rule. They protested intensely when the staff sometimes — and very deliberately — changed the order and began with the "end table," the "end bed," or the end of the "wheelchair line."

In the distinctions made by Simmel, staff who show their initiative express a tendency towards a personal subordination of patients. Patients, in their turn, react to this. If they can transform the personal initiative into an objective principle, it will also subordinate the staff. Hence, patients try to convert personal initiative into established rules.

The staff, for their part, tried hard to keep every informal arrangement from becoming entrenched. Thus, one ward applied an "every-other-day" order for its food-distribution system. "In the morning we did it the other way. So we said that now we were going to begin from the right side instead." The patients were very irritated: " 'What the heck... have you forgotten me?' They sat and yelled at us." A practical nurse described how the patients sometimes shout when these rules are not followed. She reproached herself and others on the staff for making the establishing of these orders possible:

"But often we get them used to it ourselves. I mean, if you come into a four-bed room, you take the hardest ones first, so that it's done. Then someone new comes and you say that they should start here..."

Patients' Control in Doubt

As was pointed out above, the patients made sure that the mealtime schedule was followed by the staff. They were up early, going up and down corridors in their wheelchairs. They sat in the dayroom waiting for the meal. "They're not doing anything. So they come out here when it's close to half past twelve," said one nurse.

To the patients, waiting was an important activity. They sat in their places, making sure that everything went as it should. This was *one* way of controlling the implementation of the mealtime schedule. The staff, on their part, reacted by questioning — in different ways — this activity of the patients. They criticized the patients' interest in mealtimes.

> "It seems to me that it's the highlight of the whole day. 'Now we eat breakfast. Okay, later we twiddle our thumbs until dinner.' This is how it is for the majority of patients... 'Now it will soon be breakfast, now it'll soon be dinner..' "

The staff discussed this intense interest on the part of the patients in an ironic manner. The patients did not employ their time between meals for anything "useful." They only sat. As a result, it was implied, they were hardly entitled to act as supervisors. In addition, it was suggested that the vigilance of the patients was pathetic and nothing to take seriously. In one group interview, one of the nurses said, "The food. It's what everything centers around." The others agreed.

> " 'Soon it will be coffee time' and 'I haven't gotten my coffee' and 'Now I have to go down to the corner to get a place at the table for dinner.' It is the *only* thing they have, really."

The staff said, among other things, that the patients were not really hungry. Therefore, mealtimes had lost an essential function — or, rather, they should have done so. They assumed that patients did not really need any extra energy. Patients ought not to be hungry: they hardly move and therefore burn very few calories. This fact made the patients' intense interest in meals unjustifiable. Besides, patients were said to be more interested in the event than in the food as such. One practical nurse commented:

> "I can't really believe that the patients get hungry here. When the food comes, they eat."

Conclusion

Researchers have discerned a mortification process among those admitted to total institutions (Goffman 1961, pp. 14-43; Karmel 1969, pp. 134-141). Many studies have indicated that there is minimal communication between patients in institutions. This has been explained by, among other things, the disengagement theory (Cumming & Henry 1961). A correlation has been discovered between the degree and duration of institutionalization and the lack of communication (Rosenfelt et al 1964; Coe 1965). Goffman, on the other hand, describes withdrawal behavior as being characteristic of newcomers to total institutions (1961, p. 146). It has also been emphasized how delicate a matter it is to express personal opinions (Sellerberg 1988) in the group climate which prevails in wards of this type. There is thus a series of conditions which seem to inhibit the patient's activity.

What, then, causes individuals, in these supposedly mortifying wards, to act and react in the ways described? The analysis showed that the firm time schedule subordinating both staff and patients paradoxically functioned as a factor activating collective actions and "opposite" reactions.

There is one observation which might possess some explanatory value here: the time schedule was a simple regulation pertaining to the work of the staff which was *also* available to the patients. This clarity on the part of the subordinating principle is, of course, a precondition for the patients' being able to take part in this kind of interaction and perspective contest: the rule has to be accessible to both parties.

When one party is passive, or cannot understand or stress its own perspective, there will be little need for the other to react. The interaction of "perspective expressions" then loses its rigidity and thereby its significance. As an example, one of the eight wards contained the particularly arteriosclerotic patients. It seems significant that here the staff had relaxed their ambitions when it came to maintaining a tight schedule:

"Now at dinner I had a patient who eats very slowly. But I think you have to take the time you need. You can't do anything about the fact that she can't chew big pieces."

A nurse in this ward was of the opinion that if the tray did not get on the cart on its way back to the kitchen, then it could just stay in the ward:

"I never think about the food cart being picked up. I don't even know what time they get it. It never crosses my mind out here. I have my patient. The tray will just have to stay here until the next meal and go down then for washing. It's no problem."

In this study on the wards in two Swedish hospitals, the negotiation perspective did not seem to be relevant; that would have implied a kind of "pairing" and co-ordinating of the views held by patients and staff, respectively. Instead they took sides. The results seemed to indicate that analyses of relations between staff and patients as negotiations between parties in different power positions might benefit from the contemplation of rather subtle features (Strauss 1978; Sugrue 1982, pp. 280-292; Levy 1982, pp. 293-311; Kleinman 1982, pp. 312-327; Hall & Spencer-Hall 1982, pp. 328-349). Conditions may be very slightly or not at all negotiable. The point, however, is that that which is non-negotiable has consequences, too.

Finally, however, a reservation should be made: here the positive, activating results of the fixed time schedule have been emphasized. However, this analysis concerned patients and staff as representatives of their respective groups and group perspectives. Interaction acquires another kind of significance when, for example, a patient questions the rules on his/her own, and in his/her own interests. Now, the fixed time schedule can be used by the staff against the individual patient. An LPN put forward the following line of argumentation on the basis of her staff perspective. She described how she was once asked by a patient to peel her banana — outside the schedule. In this particular case, the individual patient who wanted a banana stood alone.

"One day she rang at 11:30 and wanted me to peel a banana. I refused. 'No,' I said. 'I won't peel a banana for you.' But, yes, she wanted one, 'No,' I said, 'I can't in good conscience give you a banana. I wouldn't have done it for my kids. I wouldn't have done it at home. You can't sit and eat a banana one hour before a meal.' "

As Montesquieu (1949) once stressed, power is an ongoing process which inevitably needs new injections of strength, every day. As he wrote (p. 133), "Those who govern have a power which, in some measure, has need of fresh vigor every day." — At the two hospitals involved in this study, the superordinated mealtime schedule had actually become such a source, from which both staff and patients derived "fresh vigor" in a kind of power interaction.

Notes

1. Simmel 1964, p.250.
2. The study involved a quarter of the patients and half the staff at the respective institutions. 223 people were interviewed, 87 of whom were patients, the remaining 136 being institution staff. The interviews took place during the daytime and were often made with groups of patients (at mealtimes) and groups of staff (at coffee breaks). Night staff were not included. Some of the more senile patients were not interviewed due to the difficulty in communicating with them. The use of observational technique during mealtimes allowed non-verbal expressions to be recorded, too.
3. Roemer and Friedman believe that the American hospital system is moving in the same general direction as the European system.

III

The Opposition Has Paradoxical Consequences

9

The Paradox of the Good Buy

*... it happens that all these materials, these forces
and interests, in a peculiar manner remove
themselves from the service of life that originally
produced and employed them...*
Georg Simmel on the Autonomization of Contents

The empirical basis of this chapter consists of 50 tape-recorded interviews dealing with consumer habits in general. In these interviews individuals talked, among other things, about times when they regarded themselves as "smart" consumers. The material is described in Sellerberg (1976, 1977). These interviews will provide illustrations of my hypothesis concerning the way in which "the calculating consumer attitude" may come to operate autonomously, thereby destroying itself in the end.

In his analysis of the monetary economy and urban mentality, Simmel distinguishes factors which stimulate a calculating attitude:

"Modern mind has become more and more calculating. The calculative exactness of practical life which the money economy has brought about corresponds to the ideal of natural science: to transform the world into an arithmetic problem, to fix every part of the world by mathematical formulas. Only money economy has filled the days of so many people with weighing, calculating, with numerical determinations, with a reduction of qualitative values to quantitative ones". (Simmel 1964, p.412)

Changes in retailing have been great during the last few decades. Analyses of the effects of these changes, especially with regard to economic rationality for sellers, have been numerous. But how have price

101

tags, self service, unit pricing, etc., changed the buying situation for the consumer? One example might be mentioned: In the olden days, prices would often be established in the course of the actual purchasing process, not before. Now there are visible labels showing the price. Another way of indicating predetermined prices is to fix them to the front edge of shelves, often — as in Sweden — along with a so-called "comparison price" (the price per weight unit). This is indeed a system which encourages *quantitative comparisons.*

A second characteristic is the *rapid transformation* of the market. Prices as well as qualities are impermanent. Handbooks on retailing stress the importance of setting time limits for price offers. The transitory character of prices is emphasized in advertisements: "Bargain time at your department store."

Calculating Consumers

In an interview, a marketing man stressed an essential feature of "a good buy": "A condition of a good buy is that the difference in price or quality is *fully measurable* to me."

The interviewed consumers always described their good buys in comparative terms. "And I went to Malmö (a town about 20 miles from where the interviewee lived), and I could buy tins of drinking chocolate there for 11,50 crowns. They cost 17 crowns at home," a man said.

Buying becomes a way of saving. One man — an office worker living in a small municipality — can be quoted: "If there is a bargain price on anything, then I buy 10 of them. And maybe I save as much as 7,50 crowns. I always keep an eye on unit prices, so I can see how much I save by buying this or that."

One man — with a disability pension — argued that an individual's chief talent for cheap buying consists in possessing a good memory: "One has to remember a lot to keep in touch with the varying prices so that one gets the best pennyworth."

Interviewees described the "calculating attitude" as a state of constant vigilance and attentiveness: prices are constantly revised, special offers are always occasional.

The price-conscious consumer had to make incessant revisions. In the interviews, consumers were asked how a good consumer should act: Be curious. Read the papers. Read the advertisements. Keep a constant watch.

An elderly man (a 73-year-old engineer) talks about these new ideal characteristics on the part of a housekeeper: "Buying may be more difficult these days for housekeepers. To keep a daily watch on offers. . . Nowadays housekeepers sit with newspapers in front of them and keep an eye out for bargain offers. And my wife is quite certain that she saves a lot of money that way..."

This leads to a paradoxical feature of the situation: When entering the supermarket, the interviewed consumers expected to find "unexpected" extra offers. The interviewed consumers stressed their perpetual watchfulness, aimed at bringing their knowledge of prices up to date in every particular. "You can definitely make good buys if you're there at the right moment and are lucky, too," says a man. And frustration is the described result when the right moment is missed. A shop-assistant comments on this: "There are those poeple who don't keep their eyes open. Even if there are a hundred bags of flour in front of them, they ask me: 'Won't flour be on special offer soon?' So I have to tell them that it was last week. 'Oh, I missed that.' In other words, people must *be on their toes* if they want to buy cheaply."

A marketing man saw the expanding credit system as a factor in making more people prepared for this "right moment" and thus for unexpected good buys. Thanks to his credit card, he had himself bought pieces of furniture for 8,000 crowns which would otherwise have cost 12,000. According to him, "It's interesting to try to use the credit card system in the search for good buys."

An office worker — a man, 25 years old — believes that the credit-card system makes people less restricted in their buying opportunities. "One can make good buys," he says, "even without any money."

Some consumers seem to become veritable virtuosos in the art of good buying. They remember their good buys with an undertone of triumph. Tales are told about when, where, and how those purchases were made. These consumers compete with themselves, keen to beat their own price records: "I have never paid more than 35 crowns for one kilo of coffee," a man said, a 46-year-old clerk.

These good buys are no doubt more often the subjects of conversation than bad ones. A consequence of such word-of-mouth communications is that some people imagine themselves to be unfairly deprived: "I never ever make a real bargain. Others talk about their good buys. I happened to lay my hands on this and that and. . . That's what others say. But I never find anything. And if I go to a sale I usually come out with nothing. Even if I were to buy anything, I'm usually unhappy about it by the time I get home," said one woman, a catering assistant aged 62. To those who read the advertisements covering a large region, the offers of their own village seemed bad buys. "You can't make any real bargains in this place," one woman commented (60 years old, the wife of an industrial worker).

The Paradox of Autonomy

Modern man has been criticized for his materialism, his incessant chasing after things. In a sense, the notion could be reversed: Maybe it is not a matter of a material chase but of a hunt for the tempting occasions, for the good buys, affecting — in this case — the would-be smart consumer?

It is interesting to relate this intense striving for the good buy to Simmel's discussion of the miser and the spendthrift. The good-buyer who above all wants to make as smart a buy as possible, irrespective of the object in question, is in a sense *both* a spendthrift and a miser. The important question in Simmel's analyses is often not "to be or not to be" — but "to be *and* not to be", to be the miser *and* at the same time his polar opposite. So miserliness and prodigality are often found within the same person. But in Simmel's description this phenomenon involves different areas of interest and is connected to different moods. Thus, restlessness and calculation of prices with little interest in the object exist both in the miser *and* the spendthrift. The spendthrift is far more similar to the miser than their apparent polarization would seem to indicate. Money is as important to the spendthrift as it is to the miser, only not in the form of possessing it, but in its expenditure (Simmel 1971, p. 183). The wastrel, writes Simmel, is *not* someone who senselessly gives his money to the world. Instead, the spendthrift uses it for senseless purchases, that is, for purchases that are not appropriate to his circumstances (Simmel 1971, p. 182). In the same way as the miser, the spendthrift hence becomes indifferent to the object once he possesses it. This becomes particularly evident in primitive economies where the miserly conservation of valuables is not consistent with the nature of these valuables, that is, with the very limited storage time of agricultural produce (Simmel 1971, p. 182). To be a miser *and* a spendthrift illustrates the inevitable irony in social life: what we are really anxious to secure for ourselves may become thwarted in consequence of our very efforts. A saleswoman described the way in which good buys have come to possess an autonomous value to the customers she met, "People are like that nowadays. . . they *have* to buy if it's cheap. Even if it actually means that they lose by it."

"Shopkeepers use those 'baits', and we go off and buy things — not because we really need them, but because we look at the price and it is 2 crowns less than usual," said a 60-year-old industrial worker.

The calculating attitude is dynamic and it can only be maintained with an effort. One must not be caught napping. Action is called for. The alert consumer sets off, making cheap buys and carrying them home with a sense of jubilation - the good buy is psychologically uplifting. He or she will travel far if the price of sugar is lower some eighteen miles away. The clever purchases made by such a consumer become independent of his/ her needs. His or her smart purchases turn into good buys told about by the consumer among other good buys told about by others, in the autonomously functioning social world of calculating, comparing consumers.

Simmel describes the ever-present tendency towards an autonomization of the motives and interests that govern our behavior: They become ends in themselves, effective on the basis of their own strength and in their own right, "selective and creative quite independently of their entanglement with practical life, and not because of it" (Simmel 1964, p.42).

In Simmel's view, this tendency towards autonomization is ubiquitous. He describes it in science, and as play and sociability. Simmel also describes what he regards as the ultimate consequence — the complete reversal "from the determination of the forms by the materials of life to the determination of its material by forms that have become supreme values" (1964, p. 42). The furthest development of such a reversal is expressed by the idea: "Fiat justitia, pereat mundus" — justice be done, even if the world perishes as a result. Or, as in this less consequential case, with the contradiction of scheming subverting the ultimate goal of the scheme: We want to make bargains — even if we go bankrupt because of them.

10

The Poor of Our Time:
Objects of Enlightened Despotism

> *"...when assistance to the poor derives
> teleologically from a goal one hopes to pursue in
> this way, rather than from the causal basis of a
> real and effective unity among all the members of
> the group, the rights of the poor dwindle to
> nothingness."*
>
> Georg Simmel in Der Arme

This chapter deals with a group whose relation to society is analogous to that of the poor described by Simmel: it is concerned with geriatric patients. More particularly, it addresses the issue of the way in which these patients regard and receive their nourishment. The food for elderly geriatric-care patients in Swedish hospitals is a matter covered by regulations with nationwide applicability, and the exact vitamins and nutrients which every meal should contain are indicated very precisely. These food-intake norms are stated in *Hospital Diets (Sjukhuskoster)*, published by a coordinating committee of experts on hospital food. New norms are presented at intervals in new and revised editions of this publication. The norms are then introduced to staffs in the various counties in a more pedagogical version of *Hospital Diets*.

In effect, the norms which specify exactly what each meal should provide for each patient serve to define that patient's real position: he/she becomes a recipient, and that which is to be received has been determined not by the recipient, but by the giver. What happens to the patients' own food wishes in this situation? The question manifested itself when the author conducted an interview study among patients in geriatric care.

The starting-point of my reasoning is a comparison of two studies affecting the same group of patients. The first study referred to the exact quantity of vitamins, minerals, fiber, etc., which the patients were supposed to have at each meal (Mattisson & Frandsen 1984). In this study of geriatric patients, a dietician and a nutritionist measured the elderly patients' food intake as exactly as possible. The patients' nutritional status was also measured in different ways. In addition to weight, the TSF — Triceps skinfold — value was recorded, which entails measuring the skinfold, as well as the AMC — arm muscle circumference —, gauged with a tape measure. Further, the patients' nutritional status was ascertained by means of various laboratory tests for the hemoglobin level, serum iron, serum albumin and iron-binding proteins. Each of these measurements was thus used in order to judge to what extent the patients had reached certain nutritional norm-goals centrally defined by the medical authorities.[1,2] This has turned out to be a very common type of evaluation study.

While this nutritional investigation was taking place, the author carried out the second study — a sociological enquiry concerning the food wishes of these same patients (Sellerberg 1983).[3] The study was based on taped interviews with patients at two geriatric hospitals.[4]

The question of the food intake of the elderly was thus approached from these two very different perspectives.

In this situation, one question assumes crucial significance: Which results seem to be of the greatest relevance to those responsible for the care of this group of people? Are these senior staff primarily concerned with results that show to what extent nutritional intake agrees with central norms? Or are they chiefly interested in those results that reflect the patient's wishes with regard to various dishes, etc.?

To anyone who bears Simmel's description of the "recipient position" of the poor in mind, the answer is likely to be that interest will focus on the degree to which nutritional goals are fulfilled. If that turns out to be the case, interest in the views of patients is bound to be scant; after all, food conforming to nutritional norms may be served to the elderly — and the goals of the "giving" may be attained — independently of the patients. In contexts of this kind, interest simply by-passes patients/recipients.

Hospital Starvation: A Disgrace for the Giver

Simmel describes the shame experienced by the relatives of the poor when others were able to observe a difference in standard. The aim was to raise the poor person to the proper level. Today, when stringently-controlled diet regimes do not succeed, the difference between the nutritional level specified in the relevant norm and the actual state of things is clearly stated by way of the variety of nutritional evaluations that are being implemented. An (observable) difference seems to lead to a kind of administrative shame.

One reason for this is that such nutritional studies generally seem to attract extensive coverage. The mass media publish the differences, occasionally stigmatizing the failure to reach prescribed nutritional standards. Counties and hospitals where "hospital starvation" is found are named publicly.

Again, the reasoning in Simmel's essay comes to mind; the family or the relatives of a poor person could to a certain extent ignore his/her material standard. But when outside people observed too great a difference in standard between the poor member and the other relatives, then the family had to bear the shame (Simmel 1971).

Public Means for Public Ends

How did the recipients' own wishes fare? Did they "dwindle into nothingness"? — My study also contained staff interviews out on the wards; staff at both hospitals complained loudly about what happened to the food wishes of patients (Sellerberg 1983). They told of inflamed debates about whether the elderly could have jam with their pancakes, or whipped cream with their apple pie, when their daily quota of carbohydrates and fat was already filled. They described the sensitive situations when relatives gave elderly patients bananas (too much sugar) or chocolate (too much fat and sugar) as gifts.

It is not easy to summarize the result of the interviews with patients. Results from interviewing within total institutions have to be interpreted with care. Besides interviewing, my method was to record group discussions conducted by patients in connection with their meals. Without exception, these discussions focused on traditional dishes and eating habits: pea soup on Thursday; herring on "herring day", that is Tuesday (see chapter 8). My report on the results (Sellerberg 1983) contained many discussions by the patients about these time-honoured dishes in the Swedish home-cooking tradition.

When I reported these results of the sociological study to the appropriate county authorities, I encountered **neither** unwillingness to listen **nor** unfavorable reactions: instead I was met with confusion. What was one to do with *this* information? It did not fit in. The geriatric patients' own wishes seemed to represent an element of little pertinence. What is the relation between wishes for traditional dishes such as herring, pea soup and apple porridge on one hand, and central nutritional goals on the other? Inevitably, these wishes become irrelevant to the "giver" — the county — who is concerned with the very precise public goals, that is, the prescribed nutritional standards. Actually, the processes consist of assistance paid out of the county's funds for attaining the county's goals; as Simmel writes, "public means for public ends."

The Future

A few hypotheses regarding future developments are offered below; they were formulated on the basis of present tendencies.

First of all there are indications that public nutritional goals will become even more precise, measurements even more finely tuned. In the beginning, Swedish recommendations for hospital diet were concerned with the way in which nutritional values should be divided among meals. At that point, the only specifications were that certain meals should contain components from all the basic food categories. It was a question of balance, the aim being to ensure that the two main meals would have an equal nutritional content. The main issue then was that that balance should be the same from day to day. It was of no importance whether there was an accumulation, for example, of energy intake in the middle of the day. But specifications have greatly increased. Now, each meal has its own norm values. (In other contexts, the tendency towards a **"scientification"** of health care has been described. See Beckman 1981, Liljeström & Jarup 1983, Waerness 1984, Bergendahl 1985.)[5]

In the **second** place, there are indications that a growing number of fields are defined in exact, official norms of this type. Today, for example, the patients' feeling happy and at ease are elements which are incorporated in the official goal terminology. In training material that was distributed to staff in one of the studied county councils, the following comment was made regarding the most popular dishes among the patients: ". . . to increase the well-being of the patients, it is important that dishes such as pea soup, baked beans and cabbage soup, etc., **appear** on the menu" (my emphasis). — This, however, implies a different relation to the patients than serving these dishes because the patients wanted them.

Third, goal fulfilments often demand some form of visibility. Administrators and bystanders should be able to notice that the relevant institutions etc. are getting closer to the goal. Measurements are published, the results condemned or applauded.

In the **fourth** place, a special kind of external "meta-goals" seems to develop. Which county is best at **measuring** the levels of agreement with the various pre-established goal values? The modern hospital can be seen as the social vehicle for the rationalization of medical practice and also of diet. (See Turner 1987, p. 162.) A general tendency toward rationalization and calculation is described by both Weber and Simmel.

Fifth, not only new spheres but also new goals appear to emerge. For example, different hospitals had different so-called serving models: the canteen system, the tray system. A third model was something of a novelty, the "serving-dish system." It became apparent in discussions that hospitals operating the serving-dish system were considered more advanced. The most old-fashioned of the different models was the canteen system. A certain irritation and embarrassment could be discerned in interviews with those responsible for hospital nutrition in the central administration when the canteen system — still in use in certain hospital units — was discussed.

The **sixth** hypothesis is concerned with this last point. There was a continuous revision of centrally established guidelines. Those who were responsible for training material for hospital personnel pointed out that all the regulations for food preparation had been put into a loose-leaf notebook. This fact made it possible to constantly go in and change, adjusting and revising. In another work, the present author has described the shifting trends (Sellerberg 1987, pp. 162-164) in these nutritional norms.

A **seventh** point should also be made: developments seem to be heading in such a direction that goals are no longer formulated as guidelines or recommendations; they are turning into regulations. In an interview, a local hospital food administrator discusses the guidelines in *Hospital Diets*: "Before, we had no rules. This is our Bible."

An **eighth** question concerns the new opportunities for surveillance and control. Apparently, the question to what extent the growing number of guidelines are actually being complied with is becoming a matter of close and — it would seem — effective check-ups. Today, it is possible to computerize the nutritional contents of all meals in detail: it has duly become a routine procedure. The relevant administrators obtain quantitative proof of the extent to which a county or hospital approaches the goals.

These new measurement possibilities may account for a trend towards less lofty goal formulations. The goals may be stated in milligrams and parts per thousand. Representatives of different vocations seem to become involved in measurements, both practically and theoretically. The work behind the centrally formulated guidelines for diet was described by a hospital nutritional administrator as "originating with the theoreticians — the professors, the doctors, etc. The practitioners within the expert group then set to work and figured out how to give real strength to these guidelines."

In an interview at one of the geriatric hospitals, a nurse described such check-up measures connected with a dietary reform, "We had a dietician over us. One deciliter of this, and one and a half of that, and all that stuff." This nurse reacted very strongly, "It's like feeding livestock." The staff on the wards were supposed to assist when new systems of measurements were introduced. However, the ward personnel did not always function the way the measuring technique required. Regarding the measuring of all helpings with a particular measuring cup and spoon, one nurse said, "It doesn't work. . . instead we ask what the patients want. . ." Hence, staff out on the wards were often considered to be obstructive and reactionary by those in the central administrative authority.

A Self-Generating Process?

The points reviewed above are concerned with a hypothetic development of communication within an information system. The system consists of the centrally established nutritional norms which, it is true, concern the recipients-patients. But this system is **not** equipped for receiving— that is, absorbing and recording — extraneous information such as the wishes of those same patients. Rather, the changes within this information system seem to constitute a kind of "self-generating" process. Such changes have to do with the specification of goals and with controlling the fulfilment of those (nutritional) goals, as well as with the ceaseless production of new guidelines and, again, with measurements ensuring that the guidelines are adhered to. These factors seem to exist and develop in a social world of their own.

Notes

1. A summary of the study has been undertaken by Bertil Lindquist in *Näringsintaget inom långvården. Sammanfattning av jämförande studie mellan två långvårdskliniker*, November 1984.
2. In Brian S. Turner's discussion with Naomi Aronson, he points to the parallel between the notion of medical rationalization and the concept of "rations." "To ration is both to limit and to reckon, indicating an interesting conjunction of knowledge and power" (Turner 1985:152-153; Aronson 1984:62-65).
3. Sellerberg, Ann-Mari. *Mat på långvården*. Lund 1983.
4. Field research for the current study took place in 1983 at two Swedish geriatric hospitals, medical facilities specializing in the care of the elderly. Taped interviews and observations in the wards were conducted by a doctoral student, a registerered nurse, and the author. 223 people were interviewed, 87 of whom were patients and 136 staff. Interviews with patients were mostly group interviews during mealtimes. The size of the interview sample meant that a quarter of the patients and half the personnel at the institutions were interviewed. Night staff were not included. In addition, I made taped interviews with two county administrators working with the local introduction of the central diet norms. Most of the patients who were not included in the study could not be interviewed due to the various difficulties of communicating with them, mostly because of their arteriosclerosis. The aim of the study was to present to the administrators of the local health-care system the points of view of patients and personnel regarding mealtimes and food. A report was written summarizing the findings.
5. As others have also done, Liljeström & Jarup emphasize that such a scientific way of relating to the patients can also create a distancing from them. In this analysis, I have tried to distinguish what that distancing really implies. Several sociologically and historically inspired Swedish and Norwegian works have criticized the "professionalization" of health care. (See, for example, Martinsen 1975, 1981; Alvsvåg 1979; Martinsen & Waerness 1979; Saetre

1979; Jensen 1980; Waerness 1982.) The debate has been particularly intense in the Journal for The Norwegian Union of Nurses (Norsk Sykepleierforbunds Sykepleien).

Concluding Remarks

A diary of Simmel's contains the following well-known statement:

Ich weiss, dass ich ohne geistige Erben sterben werde (und es ist gut so). Meine Hinterlassenschaft ist wie eine in barem Gelde, das an viele Erben verteilt wird und jeder setzt sein Teil in irgendeinen Erwerb um, der seiner Natur entspricht, dem die Provenienz aus jener Hinterlassenschaft nicht anzusehen ist.

/"I know I shall die without intellectual heirs (which is just as well). The property I leave is distributed among many beneficiaries. Every one of them will put his share to use in some business that agrees with his own nature, and its provenance from that estate will not be discernible."/

Simmel's words on not leaving any intellectual heirs have been confirmed in one sense but not in another. They have been verified in that no uniform, "school-founding" canon of Simmel's theories has evolved; but the motley multitude of Simmel students who followed proved him partly wrong. Like Simmel's own work, this mixed bag of successors actually illustrates the paradoxical opposites in Simmel's analyses — not, perhaps, always by way of the discussions presented by these successors themselves; rather, the great variety found among their applications and interpretations of Simmel testifies to the validity of his paradoxical approach. In this context, a reference to Simmel's statement regarding the favourable aspects of being "misapplied" is appropriate.

Not only has Simmel been interpreted in a variety of ways; modes of application have differed, too. Some of Simmel's successors have been interpreters first and foremost, and their discussions have frequently emphasised his status as a sociological classic - or the absence of that status. Other commentators have applied Simmel's classic analyses of the metropolis, small groups, deviations, and conflicts. References to the "Americanization" of Simmel's sociology have been made in connection with these applications (Schnabel 1974). Reading Simmel has become an occupation with a very particular focus: urban sociology and research on small groups.

There has been a tendency towards the formation of "camps" separating the "users", those who have applied Simmel's ideas, from the "interpreters" of his texts. Still, both categories are concerned with trying to affix a definite meaning to Simmel's own advance interpretations. According to Deichman-Sörensen, Simmel's *Anfang einer unvollendeten Selbstdarstellung* characterizes this concern as a search for "fixed categories". Deichman-Sörensen maintains that Simmel's theories may just as well serve as an example of how a theory comes to lead a life of its own (Deichman-Sörensen 1990). In Nissen's view, Simmel's philosophy, in which truth is put to the test, amounts to restless thinking without a fixed point, consisting of ad-hoc transitions (Nissen 1925, p. 77). This paradoxical rootedness of Simmel's in the volatile and changeable is described by Kracauer in the following terms, "where previously hard boundaries were drawn, there now emerge crossings, here one thing flows into another. /—/ Everything shimmers, everything flows, everything is ambiguous, everything converges in a shifting form. It is the realm of chaos where we live" (Kracauer circa 1919-1920, p. 126).

Temporary Validity

Whatever you arrive at is temporarily valid and temporarily useful. That is the spirit in which I have drawn on Simmel's own analyses for this book. They have helped me proceed with the interpretation of my concrete investigations — of trust between the foodstuffs trade and its customers, of modern motherhood, of the guidelines regarding proper nutrition for elderly people in residential institutions, of that special form of subordination in working life that affects women. Simmel's analyses of reality have formed excellent instruments for continuing to develop the scrutiny of highly tangible empirical phenomena, taking it further. With Simmel's aid, discrete social situations can be seen to possess a singular dimension, namely the ever-present prerequisites for change and variation, the circumstances conducive to transitoriness and volatility, and it becomes clear that every situation contains the embryo of its own transformation into its opposite.

In actual fact, Simmel's analyses function as challenges to — in Deichman-Sörensen's words — think further, present fresh attempts, and look for new tendencies and allegories. To a person engaged in a pursuit along these lines, even the most trivial things will, according to Simmel (as presented by Deichman-Sörensen), be of general interest — perhaps even at the focus of it. To me, the legacy of Simmel is not the end but the beginning, a methodological and an analytical challenge.

Rudolf Heberle has emphasized — possibly overemphasized — this methodological-analytical capacity of Simmel's, claiming that "It is Simmel's method and procedure of analysis rather than the content of his findings which constitutes his unique and lasting contribution to the advancement of sociology. Thus we are confronted with the paradox that the philosopher who started out to redefine the subject matter of sociology gained his place among sociologists rather because of his methodological ideas" (Heberle 1965, p. 121).

Perhaps this overstates the case for Simmel's approach being his major contribution to sociology. More appropriately, Kracauer, who was closer to Simmel, concludes that "Simmel has exercised a broad and deep influence upon the intellectual life of his period that does not so much derive from the results as from the distinctive style of his thought" (Kracauer circa 1919-1920, p. 127).

Fashion, the striving for holiday adventure, confidence between tradesman and customer, the relationship of the modern mother with her family — these are examples of constant, indeed perpetual, interactions which express themselves in as constant attempts to achieve temporary validity. Trust is forever cutting the ground from under the feet of trust, just as adventure keeps being stripped of its adventurousness.

A Well to Be Tapped in Secret

"Of that crooked timber humanity was never built anything straight" (Kant, by way of Collingwood). To Simmel life was a variegated and contradictory business, and his writings are characterized by this very inconsistency and ambivalence of social life. The fact that Simmel himself did not aspire to the status of a classic is actually consistent with that same principle.

As Simmel saw an interplay of opposites, his latter-day interpreters perceive different aspects of things, sometimes diametrically opposed. Simmel's statements have been made to legitimize interpretations that occasionally clash outright. This is surely sufficient proof of his ambivalence. At the same time, contradictoriness embodies a kind of energy as well as paradoxical dynamics.

Interest in Simmel has varied a great deal in the course of time — or is it perhaps the openness with which that interest has been shown that has been the truly changeable factor? At times Simmel's analyses have been almost disreputable. Maybe the highly concrete utilization of Simmel has in fact remained at a more constant level in spite of this? Przywara writes that his thoughts have served as a well which could be tapped in secret (Przywara 1958, p. 224).

Perhaps Simmel did not have any proper heirs, but he did leave a contradictory legacy to many beneficiaries - itself an irony of social life. Even so, Simmel is still on the move today, having bequeathed to us an inheritance rich in irony — a blend of contradictions. It is in that spirit we accompany Simmel (quoted by Oakes 1980, p. 86) when he "set sail in search of an undiscovered land. Of course the journey will not end before I reach the unknown shore. However I will at least not share the fate of so many of my colleagues: they make themselves so comfortable on the ship that, in the final analysis, they mistake the ship itself for the new land."

Bibliography

Alberoni, Francesco. 1946. *Consumi e società*. Società editrice il Mulino, Bologna.

Alvsvåg, H. 1979. *Tör vi leve med döden?* Helse, död og sykepleie. Oslo: Universitetsforlaget.

Aronson, N. 1984. "Comment on Brian Turner's 'The government of the body: medical regimes and the rationalization of diet'." *The British Journal of Sociology,* Vol. 35.

Asplund, Johan. "Black Power?" *Sydsvenska Dagbladet Snällposten,* 17 November 1984.

Aubert, Vilhelm. 1963. "The housemaid - an occupational role in crisis," *Sociology of a Decade,* edited by Seymore Martin Lipset & Neil J Smelser. New Jersey.

Aubert, Vilhelm. 1976. "The Changing Role of Law and Lawyers in Nineteenth- and Twentieth Century Norwegian Society." *Lawyers in Their Social Setting,* edited by D N MacCormick. Edinburgh.

Barber, Bernard & Lobel, Lyle S. 1952. "Fashion in women's clothes and the American social system." *Social Forces,* Vol. 13, No. 2:124-131.

Barthes, Roland. 1960. "Le bleu est à la mode cette année." *Revue Francaise de Sociologie,* Vol 1, No 2.

Barthes, Roland. 1985. *The fashion system.* London: Cape.

Baruch, Geoffrey. 1981. "Moral Tales: Parents' Stories of Encounters With the Health Profession." *Sociology of Health and Illness* 3:275-295.

Beckman, S. 1981. *Kärlek på tjänstetid.* Arbetslivscentrum, Rapport 17, Stockholm.

Bell, Quentin. 1976. *On Human Finery.* Second edition, revised and enlarged.

Bergendahl, G. 1985. *Bildningens villkor.* Lund.

Berger, Peter & Luckmann, Thomas. 1967. *The Social Construction of Reality. A Treatise in the Sociology of Knowledge.* New York: Doubleday Anchor Books.

Blumer, Herbert. 1969. "Fashion: From class differentiation to collective selection." *The Sociological Quarterly,* Vol. 10, No. 3, Summer.

Brenninkmeyer, Ingrid. 1973. "The diffusion of fashion." In *Fashion Marketing. An Anthology of Viewpoints and Perspectives.* Edited by Gordon Wills and David Midgley. London: George Allen & Unwin Ltd.

Brown, Roger. 1967. *Social Psychology.* New York & London: The Free Press.

Burns, Tom. 1966. "The study of consumer behaviour. A sociological view." *Archives Européennes de Sociologie,* vol 7.

Burns, Tom. 1973. "Leisure in Industrial Society." In *Leisure and Society in Britain*, ed. by Michael A Smith, Stanley Parker & Cyril Smith. London: Allen Lane.

Burch, R William Jr. 1965. "The Play World of Camping: Research into the Social Meaning of Outdoor Recreation." *American Journal of Sociology*, vol LXX, 1965.

Carman, James M. 1973. "The fate of fashion cycles in our modern society." In *Fashion Marketing. An Anthology of Viewpoints and Perspectives*. Edited by Gordon Wills and David Midgley. London: George Allen & Unwin Ltd.

Coe, R. 1965. "Self-Conception and Institutionalization." In *Older People and Their Social World*, edited by A. Rose and W. Peterson. Philadelphia.

Coser, Lewis A. 1965. "Introduction." In *Georg Simmel*, edited by Lewis A Coser. Englewood Cliffs: Prentice-Hall.

Coser, Lewis. 1974. *Greedy Institutions. Patterns of Undivided Commitment.* London.

Coser, Rose Laub. 1959. "Some Social Functions of Laughter." *Human Relations* 12:171-182.

Coser, Rose Laub. 1960. "Laughter Among Colleagues." *Psychiatry* 23:81-95.

Coser, Rose Laub. 1980. "Some Functions of Laughter." In *The Pleasures of Sociology*, edited by Lewis A. Coser. A Mentor Book. (Orig. in Human Relations 12).

Cumming, E. & Henry, W. 1961. *Growing Old*. New York.

Danger, E P. 1973. "Colour trend and consumer preference." In *Fashion Marketing. An Anthology of Viewpoints and Perspectives*. Edited by Gordon Wills and David Midgley. London: George Allen & Unwin Ltd.

Deichman-Sörensen, Trine. 1990. "Ved vitenskapens grense. Utsnitt fra Georg Simmels filosofi og virkningshistorie." *Sosiologi i dag*, vol 2.

Ekendahl, Sigrid. 1942. "Några små anteckningar." In *Sveriges servitriser*, edited by Bror Abelli and Karl Otto Zamore. Stockholm. ("Some little notes," in *The waitresses of Sweden*.)

Fallers, Lloyd A. 1954 "A note on the trickle effect." *The Public Opinion Quarterly*, Autumn.

Fine, Gary A. 1983. "Sociological Approaches to the Study of Humor." Pp. 159-181 in *Handbook of Humor Research*. Vol. 1, edited by P.E. McGhee and J.H. Goldstein. New York: Springer-Verlag.

Frisby, David. 1981. *Sociological Impressionism. A Reassessment of Georg Simmel's Social Theory*. London.

Frisby, David. 1985. *Fragments of Modernity. Theories of Modernity in the Work of Simmel, Kracauer and Benjamin*. Cambridge.

Förskolan. Betänkande avgivet av 1968 års barnstugeutredning (SOU) 1972:27, Stockholm (Day-nurseries. Report from the 1968 Royal Committee. (SOU) 1972, 27, Stockholm.)

Goffman, E. 1961. *Asylums*. New York: Doubleday and Sons (Anchor Books).

Hall, P. & Spencer-Hall, D.A. 1982. *"The Social Conditions of the Negotiated Order."* Urban Life 11:328-49.

Heberle, Rudolf. 1965. "Simmel's Method." In *Georg Simmel*, edited by Lewis A Coser. Englewood Cliffs.

Henslin, James H. 1968. "Trust and the Cab Driver." *Sociology and Everyday Life*, edited by Marcello Truzzi. New Jersey: Prentice-Hall.

Horowitz, Tamar. 1975. "From élite fashion to mass fashion." *Archives Européennes de Sociologie*, Vol. 16, No. 2:283-295.

Jensen, K. 1980. "Ånd og hånd i sykepleien." *Sosiologi i dag*, Oslo, Nr 3.

Karmel, M. 1969. "Total Institution and Self-Mortification." *Journal of Health and Social Behavior*, vol 10 (June):134-141.

Kalymun, M. 1982. "Factors Influencing Elderly Women's Decisions Concerning Their Living Room Possessions During Relocation." *Ph.D. Dissertation*, Pennsylvania State University. Dissertation Abstracts International, 43:233A.

King, Charles W. 1973. "A rebuttal to the 'trickle down' theory." In *Fashion Marketing. An Anthology of Viewpoints and Perspectives*. Edited by Gordon Wills and David Midgley. London: George Allen & Unwin Ltd.

Kleinman, S. 1982. "Actors' Conflicting Theories of Negotiation." *Urban Life* 11:312-27.

Koffka, K. 1935. *Principles of Gestalt Psychology*. New York: Harcourt, Brace.

Koplin Jack, Nancy & Schiffer, Betty. 1948. "The limits of fashion control." *American Sociological Review*, vol 13.

Kracauer, Sigfried. ca 1919-1920. *Georg Simmel: Ein Beitrag zur Deutung des geistigen Leben unserer Zeit*. Unpublished manuscript. Quoted in Frisby 1981.

König, René. 1974. *A la Mode: On the social psychology of fashion*. New York: Seabury Press Inc.

Lang, Kurt & Lang, Gladys. 1961. *Collective Dynamics*. New York: Thomas Y Crowell Company.

Lantz, Sture W. 1968. *Vi serverar, I*. Hotell- och restauranganställdas organisationskrönika. Stockholm. (We wait at the table, I. An organizational chronicle for employees of hotels and restaurants.)

Lasch, Christopher. 1978. *The Culture of narcissism: American life in an age of diminishing expectations*. New York.

Levine, Donald N. 1971. "Introduction." In *Georg Simmel*. On Individuality and Social Forms, edited by Donald N Levine. Chicago and London: The University of Chicago Press.

Levine, Donald N, Carter, E.B. & Gorman, E.M. 1976. "Simmel's Influence on American Sociology." *American Journal of Sociology*, vol 81.

Levy, J.A. 1982. "The Staging of Negotiations Between Hospice and Medical Institutions." *Urban Life* 11:293-311.

Lichtblau, Klaus. 1986. "Die Seele und das Geld. Kulturtheoretische Implikationen in Georg Simmels Philosophie des Geldes." *Kölner Zeitschrift für Soziologie und Sozialpsychologie*, Sonderheft 27.

Lifton, Robert Jay. 1971. "Protean Man." *Archives of General Psychiatry*, Vol. 24.

Liljeström, R. & Jarup, B. 1983. *Vardagsvett och vetenskap i vårdarbetet*. Svenska Kommunalarbetarförbundet, Stockholm.

Lindquist, B. 1984. *Näringsintaget inom långvården. Sammanfattning av jämförande studie mellan två långvårdskliniker*. Lund.

Lo-Johansson, Ivar. 1966. *Kungsgatan*. Stockholm.

Luhmann, Niklas. 1979. *Trust and Power*. Chichester: John Wiley and Sons.
Martinsen, K. 1975. *Sykepleie og filosofi*. Stensilserie nr 35, Filosofisk Institutt, Universitetet i Bergen.
Martinsen, K. 1981. "Omsorgens filosofi og omsorg i praksis." *Sykepleien*, Nr 8.
Martinsen, K. & Waerness, K. 1979. *Pleie uten omsorg?* Oslo: Pax.
Mattisson, I & Frandsen, B. 1984. *En kostundersökning inom långvården i Malmöhus läns landsting*. Augusti.
Mayntz, Renate & Nedelmann, Birgitta. 1987. "Eigendynamische Soziale Progresse. Anmerkungen zu einem analytischen Paradigma." *Kölner Zeitschrift für Soziologie und Sozialpsychologie*.
Merton, R K. 1957. *Social Theory and Social Structure*. New York: Free Press.
Midgley, David. 1973. "The Seamless Stocking Saga." In *Fashion Marketing. An Anthology of Viewpoints and Perspectives*. Edited by Gordon Wills and David Midgley. London: George Allen & Unwin Ltd.
Montesquieu, de Secondat, C.L. 1949. *The Spirit of the Laws*. Translated by T. Nugent and with an introduction by F. Neumann. New York: Haffner.
Moreland, Carol P. 1978. "Simmel: Embodiment of the Dialectic." *Quarterly Journal of Ideology*, vol 2-3.
Morgan, D. 1982. "Failing Health and the Desire of Independence: Two Conflicting Aspects of Health Care in Old Age." *Social Problems* 30.
Munthers, Q J. 1977. "Social stratification and consumer behaviour." *The Netherlands' Journal of Sociology*, vol 13.
Möbler & Miljö (Furniture & Environment). 1977, No.3:7.
Nedelmann, Birgitta. 1987. "Georg Simmel as an Analyst of Autonomous Processes: The Merry-Go-Round of Fashion." Paper presented to the Symposium Georg Simmel and Contemporary Sociology, Boston University, Department of Sociology.
Nissen, Ingjald. 1925. "Vergesellschaftung als Einstellung. Eine Betrachtung zu Simmels Soziologie." In *Annalen der Philiosophie und philosophischen Kritik*, edited by Hans Vaihinger and Raymund Schmidt. Leipzig.
Nystroem, Paul H. 1928. *The Economics of Fashion*. New York.
Oakes, Guy. 1980. "Introduction." In *Georg Simmel's Essays on Interpretation in Social Science*, translated and with an introduction by Guy Oakes. Manchester: Rowman and Littlefield.
Orbdlik, A.J. 1942. "Gallows Humor: A Sociological Phenomenon." *American Journal of Sociology* 47:709-716.
Persson, Malin. 1977. *Vissa aspekter på den illegala ekonomiska marknaden - Förundersökning utförd av Brottsförebyggande rådet*. Department of Sociology, University of Lund.
Persson, Rune & Dahlgren, Anita. 1978. *Ungdomars konsumtion*, Statens Ungdomsråd, Stockholm. (The Consumption of Young People, The National Youth Council.)
Pogrebin, Mark R. & Poole, Eric D. 1988. "Humor in the Briefing Room. A Study of the Strategic Uses of Humor Among Police." *Journal of Contemporary Ethnography*. Vol. 17:183-210.
Poggi, Gianfranco. 1979. "Introduction. Niklas Luhmann's Neo-Functionalist

Approach: An Elementary Presentation." in *Niklas Luhmann Trust and Power*. Chichester.

Prus, Robert C. 1975. "Resisting Designations: An Extension of Attribution Theory into a Negotiated Context." *Sociological Inquiry* Vol 45(1):3-14

Przywara, Erich. 1958. "Erinnerungen an Georg Simmel von Erich Przywara." In *Buch des Dankes an Georg Simmel. Briefe, Erinnerungen, Bibliographie. Zu seinem 100. Geburtstag am 1. März 1958*, edited by Kurt Gassen & Michael Landmann. Berlin.

Radcliffe-Brown, A.R. 1940. "On Joking Relationships." *Africa* 13:195-210.

The 1969 Report. *Om sexuallivet i Sverige* (SOU) 1969:2, Stockholm. (Sexual life in Sweden, The 1969:2 Report, Stockholm)

Reynold, William H. 1968. "Cars and clothing: understanding fashion trends". *Journal of Marketing*, vol 32, July.

Richardson, Jane & Kroeber, A.L. 1940. "Three centuries of women's dress fashions." *Anthropological Records*, vol 5, no 2.

Robinson, Dwight E. 1958. "Fashion Marketing." *Harvard Business Review*, vol 36, no 6.

Roemer, M.I. & Friedman, J.W. 1978. "The World Scene in Doctor-Hospital Relations." In *Dominant Issues in Medical Sociology*, edited by H.D. Schwartz and C.S. Kart. New York: Random House.

Rosenfelt, R., Kastenbaum, R. & Slater, P. 1964. "Patterns of Short-Range Time Orientation in Geriatric Patients." In *New Thoughts on Old Age*, edited by R. Kastenbaum. New York: Springer.

Roth, J.A. 1963. *Timetables: Structuring the Passage of Time in Hospital Treatment and Other Careers*. Indianapolis: Bobbs-Merrill.

Roth, J.A. 1984. "Staff-Inmate Bargaining Tactics in Long-Term Treatment Institutions." *Sociology of Health and Illness* 6:111-131.

Rubenstein, Robert. 1987. "The Significance of Personal Objects to Older People." *Journal of Aging Studies*. Vol. 1, No 3:225-238.

Rykwert, Joseph. 1977. "On strata in the kitchen, or the archeology of tasting." In *The anthropologist's cookbok* edited by Jessica Kuper. London: Routledge and Kegan.

Sapir, Edward. 1931. "Fashion." In *Encyclopedia of the Social Sciences*, vol VI. New York.

Saetre, T. 1979. *Profesjonsideologi som årsak til lav yrkesaktivitet blant norske sykepleiere*. Hovedfagsoppgave, Sosiologisk Institutt, Bergen.

Schnabel, Peter-Ernst. 1974. *Die soziologische Gesamtkonzeption Georg Simmels*. Stuttgart.

Sellerberg, Ann-Mari. 1973. *Kvinnorna på den svenska arbetsmarknaden under 1900-talet. En sociologisk analys av kvinnornas underordnade position i arbetslivet*. CWK Gleerup Bokförlag AB, Lund.

Sellerberg, Ann-Mari. 1975a. "The Life of Young Working-Class Mothers in Sweden." *Journal of Marriage and the Family*, May.

Sellerberg, Ann-Mari. 1975b. "Sociological features of women's work." *Sociale Wetenschappen*, 18e Jaargang, Nr 4, 1975, pp. 250-262.

Sellerberg, Ann-Mari. 1976a. *En sociologisk analys av konsumtionsvanor. En intervjuundersökning av några olika konsumentgrupper 1975.* University of Lund. (A sociological analysis of consumer habits. A survey among six consumer groups, 1975. Only in Swedish.)

Sellerberg, Ann-Mari. 1976b. "On the Differing Social Meanings of Consumption." *Journal of the Market Research Society*, 18, 4, 1976.

Sellerberg, Ann-Mari. 1977. *Hur kunden möter affären. En sociologisk analys av relationen mellan konsument och affär.* Lund.

Sellerberg, Ann-Mari. 1978. *Konsumtionens sociologi.* Stockholm: Scandinavian University Books.

Sellerberg, Ann-Mari. 1979. *Moden. Sociologiska analyser av dagens heminredning.* Department of Sociology, University of Lund, Sweden.

Sellerberg, Ann-Mari. 1982. *Några sociologiska analyser av matens moden.* Department of Sociology, University of Lund, Sweden.

Sellerberg, Ann-Mari. 1983. *Mat på långvården.* (On Food in Geriatric Hospitals). Department of Sociology, University of Lund.

Sellerberg, Ann-Mari. 1984. "The Practical. Fashion's latest conquest." *Free Inquiry in Creative Sociology*, Vol. 12, No. 1.

Sellerberg, Ann-Mari. 1986. "Långvården och en sociologisk klassiker," *Tvärsnitt* 1:36-41.

Sellerberg, Ann-Mari. 1987. *Avstånd och attraktion. Om modets växlingar.* Stockholm: Carlssons förlag.

Sellerberg, Ann-Mari. 1989. "Nutritional norms in Long-Term Care. Analyzed from a Simmelean Perspective." *Acta Sociologica*, Vol 32:275-281.

Sherman, E. & Newman, E.S. 1977. "The Meaning of Cherished Personal Possessions for the Elderly." *International Journal of Aging and Human Development* 8:181-192.

Simmel, Georg. 1907. *Philosophie des Geldes.* Leipzig.

Simmel, Georg. 1923. "Der Begriff und die Tragödie der Kultur." In *Philosophische Kultur.* Potsdam.

Simmel, Georg. 1957. "Fashion." *The American Journal of Sociology*, LXII, May, reprinted from International Quarterly, October 1904.

Simmel, Georg. 1964. *The Sociology of Georg Simmel.* Translated, edited and with an introduction by Kurt H. Wolff. New York: Free Press.

Simmel, Georg. 1965. *Essays on Sociology, Philosophy & Aesthetics* by Georg Simmel et al, edited by Kurt H Wolff. New York: Harper Torchbooks.

Simmel, Georg. 1965. "The Adventure." In Kurt H Wolff (ed) *Essays on Sociology, Philosophy and Aesthetics* by Georg Simmel et al. New York: Harper Torchbooks.

Simmel, Georg. 1971. *Georg Simmel. On Individuality and Social Forms,* edited by Donald N Levine. Chicago and London: The University of Chicago Press.

Simmel, Georg. 1971. "The Poor." In *Georg Simmel. On Individuality and Social Forms,* edited by Donald N Levine. Chicago and London: The University of Chicago Press. (Orig. published as "Der Arme" in *Soziologie.* Munich and Leipzig: Dunker & Humblot, 1908.)

Simmel, Georg. 1973 "Fashion." In *Fashion Marketing, an anthology of viewpoints and perspectives,* edited by Gordon Wills and David Midgely. London: George Allen & Unwin.

Simmel, Georg. 1978. *The Philosophy of Money*. Translated by Tom Bottomore and David Frisby. London: Routledge & Kegan.

Sjukhuskoster 1982 (Hospital Diets 1982). Uppsala.

Strauss, A. 1978. *Negotiations*. San Fransisco: Jossey Bass.

Sugrue, N.M. 1982. "Emotions as Property and Context for Negotiations." *Urban Life* 11:280-292.

Susman, Margarete. 1958. "Erinnerungen an Georg Simmel." In *Buch des Dankes an Georg Simmel. Briefe, Erinnerungen, Bibliographie. Zu seinem 100. Geburtstag am 1. März 1958*, edited by Kurt Gassen & Michael Landmann. Berlin.

Svenskt Yrkeslexikon, 1965, Del II, Kungliga Arbetsmarknadsstyrelsen. Helsingborg. (Swedish occupational lexicon. National Board of Labor.)

Tarde, Gabriel. 1903. *The Laws of Imitation*. New York.

Trumpeten, Tidning för trafikrestaurangers anställda. (The Trumpet. Staff magazine for employees in the Railway Restaurants.)

Turner, Brian S. 1985. "More on the government of the body." *The British Journal of Sociology*, 36(2).

Turner, Brian S. 1987. *Medical Power and Social Knowledge*. Sage Publications.

Waerness, K. 1982. *Kvinneaspekter på sosialpolitikken*. Oslo: Universitetsforlaget.

Waerness, K. 1984. "The rationality of caring." *Economic and Industrial Democracy*, 5.

Webb, B. & Stimson, G. 1976. "People's Accounts of Medical Encounters." In *Studies in Everyday Medical Life*, edited by M. Wadsworth and D. Robinson. London: Martin Robertson.

Weber, Max. 1968a. *Economy and Society*. Vol 1. New York: Bedminster Press.

Weber, Max. 1968b. *Economy and Society*. Vol 2. New York: Bedminster Press.

Welander, Thomas. 1972. *Georg Simmel. Några synpunkter på en "dialektisk" sociologi*. Mimeographed paper, department of sociology, University of Lund.

Wilson, Elisabeth. 1985. *Adorned in Dreams: Fashion and Modernity*. Virago.

Wolff, Kurt H. 1964 "Introduction." In *The Sociology of Georg Simmel*, edited by Kurt H Wolff. New York: The Free Press of Glencoe.

Young, Agnes Brook. 1937. *Recurring Cycles of Fashion 1760-1937*. London: Harper & Row.

Zerubavel, Eviatar. 1981 a. *Hidden Rhythms*. Schedules and Calendars.

Zerubavel, Eviatar. 1981 b. "If Simmel Were A Fieldworker: On Formal Sociological Theory And Analytical Field Research." *Symbolic Interaction*, vol 3.

Ziehe, Thomas. 1984. "Kulturell friställning och narcissistisk sårbarhet." In *Ungdomskultur: Identitet och motstånd*. Stockholm.

Index